Word in the Heart

Teacher's Manual
Junior
Year 5: Quarters 1-4

Table of Contents

ISBN 10: 1-58427-296-1

ISBN 13: 978-158427296-0

Notes

An Educator Talks About Your Junior Student

A teacher must understand his students in order to succeed in their instruction and to accomplish what is needed with them and the Kingdom of God. Study each student individually and try to understand his personal and individual needs and then consider the group as a whole so that you may instruct them more effectively.

Physical Characteristics

Physically your students are strong, healthy, and alert. They are active and exuberant and, with the normal energy of those in grades four, five, and six, may amaze you with their vitality. At this age they are beginning to experiment in independence and to attempt greater degrees of personal freedom and individual rights. They may be inclined to be less tidy than you would prefer—expecially the boys—and more interested in being outside and active than sitting in a classroom.

Mental Characteristics

Mentally they are exceedingly alert, and the brightest may challenge even the best of teachers with thought-provoking questions and comments. Your students will be able to find Bible references, answer workbook questions, and read and explain Bible verses in class. Memorizing is done easily at this age and should be encouraged at every class period. They are eager for information, but will be critical and questioning and you should be ready to prove every point with Scripture. Your students can be creative, if you give them your time, interest, and understanding. They will be interested in projects that will enhance their Bible knowledge. Their interest spans and powers of concentration have improved considerably over the primary level student.

Social Characteristics

Socially your students are becoming discriminating. They will tend to separate into small groups—especially girls with girls and boys with boys. The boys will strongly prefer the male companions and pretend great dislike for girls. They will be embarrassed if strongly urged to work with girls. They can be encouraged to high standards and will expect complete fairness in all treatment. At this age, they must be taught at every opportunity to respect all authorities that are over them. Bible stories that emphasize action, courage, and obedience to God will make the deepest impressions on them.

Spiritual Characteristics

Spiritually your students are at an age to understand the necessity of obedience to God and to learn the doctrinal truths about salvation. They will respond easily to the necessity of growing in Christ and may become interested in encouraging others of their family and friends to become Christians. They need encouragement to daily devotions that include Scripture reading and prayer. They also need the very best example of Christianity that you as the teacher are able to set before them and any hypocrisy on your part will be quickly detected by the student and irreparable damage may be done to his spiritual development.

As a teacher, your life and the teachings of God's word will be under careful scrutiny by the whole class, and any failure or inconsistency on your part will be detected and exposed. "Take heed to yourself and to the doctrine. Continue in them, for in doing this you will save both yourself and those who hear you" (1 Tim. 4:16).

—Louis W. Garrett, Ph.D.

Notes

Lesson 1

Israel in Egypt

This quarter you are taking your class on an adventure of travel which they will enjoy. Juniors like this kind of study and it is not difficult to keep the classes interesting and lively with proper preparation. Here are some suggestions for you to consider that will help you to enjoy this study.

The first lesson will be different from the others because you are introducing the work for the quarter and teaching lesson one. Do not neglect this initial introduction because it is most important to the students. You will want to do these two things:

First, look over and be familiar with the whole book and introduce the class to the study as a whole. They need to know where they are beginning and where they are going. Cover briefly all they will study including a brief review of Genesis and show that there is a period of silence of about 300 years between Genesis and Exodus. The introduction inside the front cover will help you here.

Secondly, with Genesis 15:12-16 as a text, help the class see the very detailed prophecy of what you are going to study. After reading it, ask them questions like these to pinpoint their attention on the main facts. Where will they be a stranger? What will happen to them there? How long will it be? Will they leave that land? How shall they come out? How many generations will pass before they come out? Get the class to see that they are going to see this prophecy of God fulfilled in this quarter before their very eyes.

Teaching Lesson One

In this and other lessons, you are going to need a good map for the whole class to see. It will be a map of Egypt and the Wilderness. Use this every week and let the students point out where the events of the lesson occur. Another real help along with the map would be a copy of *Baker's Bible Atlas* or any good Bible atlas. This is for your own use and preparation and will aid you in understanding the land better so you can make your comments more interesting. If you need a commentary, the one by Adam Clarke is good especially on the Old Testament.

This lesson will cover more ground (six chapters) than most of these lessons and the students will not have read all of this. Most will likely know the story nevertheless, so break the lesson up into three segments and let three students tell the story in their own words. Review it yourself to touch any parts they missed and then check the students' books, answering any questions they may have. There will often be a student or two who have not filled out the book or studied their lesson. If this becomes a habit, talk with the parents urging them to help the child or encourage him.

Students like to draw at this age so have paper available for them and while looking at the large map have them draw the outline of

Egypt, the Red Sea, and the Wilderness. Have them locate Mt. Horeb or Sinai.

In case a student wants to know the five questions Moses asked God, they are found in Exodus 3:11, 13; 4:1, 10, 13. If you run short of material be ready to discuss these.

Beside preparing their lesson for next week, assign each in the class to bring a picture or draw a picture of something they think of when they think of Egypt. That's all. More "Tips" next time.

Notes

Remember last week you were to assign each pupil the homework of getting a picture of something they would think of when they hear the word "Egypt." Be sure to follow through with any special assignment like this you make. It is especially important to the pupils because some may have put a lot of time to it. Have them explain their picture and tell what they think of it. If some bring modern pictures of events going on there today, that will be fine. This will be a good chance for you to impress on their minds that the story they are studying in the Bible was real, not a fairy tale, and the land there now is exactly the land where the Israelites and the Pharaohs lived. If someone brings a picture of the Pyramids or Sphinx, you might point out that these were in Egypt when Moses lived and he likely saw them himself. Be prepared to give them some special assignment each week apart from their lesson preparation and student work. Give them ten extra points credit for a good job. If you have never done this as a teacher, you might find it very helpful in getting the class started with *interest*. What really happens is this: They are starting the class themselves with their work. This gets their interest immediately. If you have bulletin board space available have these pictures posted.

When you get ready to move into today's lesson, connect it with the last one by a review of how we "travelled" a number of places last week. Do not review by telling the whole story over again. You might do it with ten short and "to the point" questions answered quickly by the pupils. Ask specific questions to specific pupils. Or you might try this for variety. Just state a word such as, "Bush," "Zipporah," "fled," "Jethro"; use any key word of last week's lesson and have them to tell you something about that word and how it related to the lesson. When the review is over, you are ready to begin today's lesson.

Today's Lesson

This lesson is almost as long as last week's and the student has read very little of it from the Bible. Furthermore, much of the biblical detail has been omitted from the lesson text so your job is to be thoroughly familiar with these five chapters and fill in the details for your age group. There are four very good topics to be ready to discuss: (1) the plagues themselves, (2) the purpose for them, (3) the compromises attempted by Pharaoh, and (4) the hardening of Pharaoh's heart.

The Plagues: The lesson text deals mainly with this since the subject was Power of God. You would want to check the book with the pupils here covering all the miracles briefly and discussing questions they will likely have. Give them plenty of opportunity to ask questions. This is a question-asking age.

The Purpose of the Plagues: This is one of the most important points to drill home in this lesson. Three were specifically stated in the lesson: to free Israel, to convince Pharaoh that there was none like

Him, and from these miracles His name might spread throughout the world. At this point in history nobody knew much of anything about the God or gods of this slave nation other than what these Israelites might have told them. God had not shown Himself, demonstrated His power, or given His name as it was revealed to Moses. Even Moses had to be convinced. Just as the miracles of Jesus were evidence of his Divinity, these miracles of God in the form of plagues upon the Egyptians served several purposes. The one most emphasized was their purpose in proving God's power, greatness, longsuffering, and care for His people. Because of these events in Egypt, the world was going to hear about and know the God of the Israelites. Emphasize this purpose in these miracles (7:5, 17; 8:22, 23; 9:14-16).

Pharaoh's Compromises: Pharaoh did not want to do what God said. But when the plagues came, he tried to get out from under these punishments by compromising with God. Emphasize that this never works. Scriptures show the progression of a compromising spirit in Pharaoh (8:25 – in the land,"; 10:8-11 – "you who are men,"; 10:24 – "let your flocks and your herds be kept back"). The answer was "No!" each time. God does not compromise. Have three of the students pick out these scriptures and read them. Explain what a "compromise" is and let them see if they can identify them.

The Hardened Heart: This is a more difficult subject to cover adequately with the younger students especially because it involves an abstract and subjective activity of the mind. It also is difficult because sometimes it is said God hardened Pharaoh's heart, sometimes that Pharaoh hardened his own heart, and sometimes simply it was hardened. Here is an example of each. Students may read before discussing this: 9:35, 7:3, 13; 8:15, 32. This may help in explaining the topic. Anything that is hard does not give or is not changed. Illustrate with a hard ball of some kind. Then use a soft ball to show you can change it. Man's mind is like the soft ball or hard ball. God wants to be able to speak to a man's mind and have it change to do His will. You push on a ball to change it but God speaks to the mind to change it. Now when a man refuses to change and do God's will, he has "hardened his heart" before God. This is not hard to see but it is difficult for some to see how God hardened Pharaoh's heart. Think of this. If God had never spoken to Pharaoh would his heart have been hardened? No. How then did God harden it? By simply asking Pharaoh to let Israel go. This was all God did. This was God's part. Then Pharaoh said, "No!" He heard God's law and, of his own will, he refused. Therefore, he hardened his own heart. But since he could not have done this without God giving him His law or instructions to release Israel, God also hardened his heart. This will help if you have enough time to discuss this point.

For the third lesson have the students bring a picture they have drawn or cut from a publication to illustrate one of the plagues. You might assign different students different plagues so they will not all bring a locust or fly.

Have a good class. You have lots of material in this lesson to work with. More "Tips" next time.

Notes

Lesson 3

Deliverance From Bondage

As the classes continue, more material is building up for review. There is nothing that aids the learning process more than *review*. With it, you prod the memory and fix more firmly in the mind important points. Never neglect the values in review and do it regularly. Pick out five to ten good questions from the previous two lessons and ask them. Always make the questions specific and to a particular student. Otherwise, you will have one or two students answering all the questions.

If you have asked the students to do anything special for today's class, be sure you take care of it sometime during the lesson. If you have not asked but someone has volunteered to do something special, give ample time and appreciation to it. This will encourage others to act on their own.

Map Introduction: Today for the first time, the children of Israel travel. Now is the time to have the students turn to the map in their books (p. 56) and explain important points to them. You can do this best by securing a large map of the area. Let them follow in their books as you point out interesting things on the large map. You will do well to find a copy of *Baker's Bible Atlas* or some other good Bible Atlas and read about some of the features of the wilderness area. Here is where the children of Israel will spend the rest of their time during this quarter of study. Point out some approximate distances so the students can get a feel for the time involved and the area covered. If you have no access to an atlas, the distance from Egypt to the Dead Sea is 200 miles and from the Mediterranean Sea to the Southern tip of the Sinai peninsula is about 225 miles. Since you are doing this at the beginning of the class, do not point out today's journey at this time. To excite their interest tell the students you will do this at the end of today's class. Emphasize the need for them to keep their books in good shape so they will have the map to work with.

Today's Lesson: There is more student work in this lesson than in any of the previous ones. Allow more time for this when you prepare for the class.

The students today have read Exodus 12:1-14 and other scattered scriptures. Therefore, you will need to be very familiar with the other material in chapters 12-14 for discussion.

If I were teaching this lesson I would first write on the board this statement, "The Four P's." Then write under this statement one of these four words at a time and discuss them. This is the outline of the section you are studying. The words: PASSOVER, PLAGUE, PURSUIT, PRAISE. This will be easy for them to remember and they have the section outlined in their mind.

When you discuss the Passover, do the work in the book for that section. As you move to the other points, do any work in the text that they have filled in. One of the best ways to do the work within the text with as little confusion as possible is to let each pupil read a whole sentence.

Do the "Fun and Learn by Doing" last and then since they have given the names of the places where Israel traveled, locate them on the map and have them, with the use of a colored pencil, make a line indicating about where they started and where they are at the end of this lesson. They will like this.

As an object lesson, bring a road map of some state. Show it to them and let them tell you what it is. Then ask them if the Israelites had a road map with them to show them where they were going. Of course they did not have the kind of map you have. But they did have a guide to direct them. Ask them what it was. It was, of course, the pillar of cloud and fire directed by God.

Another interesting activity is to ask one or two of the students to tell what preparations they usually make when they leave home to take a vacation trip. Ask what they take with them, etc. Then ask if they know what the Israelites had with them. You might read Exodus 12:34-39 for the answer. To say the least, they traveled light.

Lessons For Today:

One: When men put their faith and trust in God they always come out victorious.

Two: We should never forget to be thankful for all God does for us.

Three: Anyone choosing to oppose God as Pharaoh did always ends in defeat. Our God will not be overcome. More timely "Tips" next time. Hope they are proving to be helpful.

Notes

We are still covering several chapters in Exodus with each lesson, so the student will have a limited understanding of the whole story. Read over all the material sufficiently to be familiar with it for class discussion. In this lesson, for example, there was not room to cover the last chapter of the lesson, so some time should be spent showing how the work of judging the problems of the people was to be arranged.

Teach Geography Now

Usually the study of Bible history and geography is left for the Senior High or Adult ages. By this time, most students studying the Bible regularly will have gone over all the history of the Bible and they needed some good explanations of the geography of the countries earlier. One of the great aids to remembering is association of an event with a place on the map that can be pointed out. If a black board is available in your classroom be sure to use it. Draw a large map of the wilderness on it and locate the various places the Israelites will visit. Place a dot for the place and a line for the name of the place to be written in. It will be worth more to the students to have each of them locate one or more of these places and write it on the board. If you have more students than places, erase the places and let new students write the names in again. Show them any pictures of the area you have access to. Much material is available on the internet. Just do a search on the name of the place to find information and images to use in class. In last week's Tips some very helpful books were mentioned. Each has a map in the student's workbook (p. 56) so let them keep up to date with where they are and with what happens at each place.

Today's lesson centers around four stops on the way to Sinai. Rephidim, the last stop, is in the mountain chain, Horeb, near the specific peak of the mountain called Sinai. At each of these stops, different things happened. Drill the class on these. They can learn them easily, especially if the event or events are written on the board beside the names of the places.

But, most of all, in today's lesson is the importance of believing God without reservation and trusting Him to keep His word. He always does. One word that stands out in the lesson is the disposition of the Israelites toward God that revealed itself in *murmuring*. In Hebrews 3:8-19 God recalls this period of Hebrew history and specifically identifies the trouble as *unbelief*. This is an excellent lesson to show how God always keeps His promises and provides our needs as well. We have different needs and He provides for them in different ways. At this time their blessings were mainly physical in food and water, but they were soon to see God promise and provide great spiritual blessings and promises at Sinai. Likewise, our blessings are both physical and spiritual.

Teacher Training Materials

If you would like some good material on improving teaching in the classroom, here are a few recommendations. *A Generation That Knows Not God* is a a teacher training manual written by Bob and Sandra Waldron. This is an excellent book discussing serveral aspects of teaching including: stressing the Bible story, lesson preparation, the use of aids, discipline in the classroom, identifying learning levels of different age groups, and more. *The Seven Laws of Teaching*, written by John Milton Gregory, offers a clear and concise presentation of the fundmental laws of teaching that have been studied and applied in a variety of educational situations. Although *Teaching Kids About God* is written for parents, this book identifies an age-by-age plan that will help teachers develop age appropriate lesson plans.

  * These, or any other teaching aids, may be purchased from the bookstore which supplies this literature.

The Creative Bible Teacher

always obeys

The Seven Laws of Teaching

1. **The teacher must know that which he would teach.**

2. **The teacher must help the student to attend with interest to the lesson being taught.**

3. **The teacher must teach in a language understood by the student.**

4. **The teacher must begin with the known and proceed to the unknown.**

5. **The teacher must excite and guide the self-activities of the student.**

6. **The teacher must aim at getting the student to reproduce the WORD IN THE HEART.**

7. **The teacher must complete, test, and confirm his work by review and application.**

These laws are explained in detail in *The Seven Laws of Teaching*, by Milton Gregory.

Notes

This lesson contains less reading material from the Bible than any previous lesson. You also have less material to work with in preparing for the class, but that should present no problem. In a lesson like this, if you seem to run short on material this is a good time to have a good review of the lessons up to this point. Pick out ten or fifteen questions on the highlights of previous lessons and have them ready if you need them near the end of the class. It is always a good practice to review often regardless of the reason for it.

An Important Step

In Exodus 19, God, for the first time, made a direct approach to Israel to see if they were willing to follow Him. Verses 3-8 record this approach. Study this section carefully. With the class you might present it clearly under three headings. First, the conditions of the covenant are stated. Israel is to agree to obey the voice of God and to keep His covenant. Here you may discuss what a covenant is and what it means to obey and to keep another's word. Secondly, the promises on God's part of what He will make of them. They will be to Him a "peculiar," or special treasure, a kingdom of priests unto Him and an holy nation. Of Christians, very similar language is found in 1 Peter 2:9, 10. As a "treasure," God is signifying their value to Him. As a "kingdom of priests," He indicates their constant access to Him. Heaven's doors are always open to their worship and petitions. As a "holy nation," He shows the character they are to maintain by obedience. You must put a chart on the board like this to make it clear to the class and show a destinction between the three statements.

"peculiar treasure" — Their Value
"kingdom of priests" — Their Access
"holy nation"—Their Character

Thirdly, all of the above would be to no avail unless Israel agreed to the conditions and promises. They did agree. This was the first formal step taken to bind Israel to God and when the agreement was made, the foundation for the *covenant between God and Israel was laid.*

God then proceeded to make preparations for the giving of the Law. To show how He expected the people to show their respect for Him, He had a boundary or some kind of markers set up and the people were not to go beyond them to reach the Mountain. They were also to purify and sanctfy themselves. This might be more difficult to discuss and explain to the younger students of the class than anything else in the lesson, since today there is no such thing as a ceremonial cleansing as was involved here. You might just explain it by saying the people were to do what God wanted them to do to be as holy and good as possible. They were to "sanctify" themselves or set themselves aside to God's word and work for the special events that were about to occur.

Another description of this great event at Sinai when God came down upon it is recorded in Hebrews 12:18-21. This was to convince the people of His power and also to convince them that they should listen to what Moses said because He was with him (v. 9). The people were really frightened by this great and unusual demonstration of power and were now ready to receive the Law God was about to give. This is a lesson about the preparation of the people who were to receive the Law now. We will study the beginning of the giving of the Law in the next lesson.

The children of Israel travel but a short distance in this lesson between two points: Rephidim to Sinai. However, take time with the students to mark this on their maps if they have not already done so. This is the tenth stop specifically mentioned in their exodus from Egypt. At Sinai they will pitch camp for a long time—one year.

Assignment for next time: When the students have prepared their lesson for next week on the Ten Commandments, have each of them bring a picture or have a true story to tell of someone breaking one of the Commandments.

More "Tips" next time.

Notes

In preparing and presenting today's lesson, there are three things to keep in mind. These may also serve as a logical outline for your classroom work.

Historical Setting: The students are studying these lessons with a time lapse between classes, but the material covered in the lesson today happened at the same time as the last lesson. Tie these lessons together very closely. One of the best ways to do this is by a good review of some of the points in the lesson last week, especially in the latter part of that lesson. Have the children of Israel at the base of the Mount waiting and Moses coming down to warn them again not to touch it. It is at this time that God speaks and gives the Ten Commandments. As He ends, the people have both seen all the miracles surrounding the Mount and heard God.

Also a part of the historical setting is still the fact that we are dealing with one nation and God. This law is being given to the Israelites and to no other nation. It is not our law today.

Memory Work: Each week a key verse in the lesson is selected for the memory verse. But, occasionally there is more that needs to be memorized than just a single verse. In today's lesson, time should be spent in class working on this. The students have a section of their lesson today where they are to be graded on memory work. So some work will already have been done on this. A good way to approach this method of study is to divide the material to be memorized into short sections or groups if you are dealing with words. A good place to divide the commandments for memory is after the fourth commandment. Work with the first four and then the last six. You might want to break up this into two periods and have something else in between as a rest for the students.

Understanding Is Most Important: In the learning process for any student, memory work has its place but it is not the most important step by far. More important than memory is understanding. This should be done well enough that a student can tell you in his own words what the commandments mean. When this can be done, he understands them. So, part of your work today is going to be explaining the meaning of the commandments and helping the students understand them. Some of the obvious ones they already know. However, study them well yourself so you can answer any questions the students might have.

Last week, you were encouraged to assign each pupil the task of bringing to class a picture or have a true story to tell of someone breaking one of the commandments. Be sure and take time to let them present what they have done. This will be a good way of explaining what the commandments really teach by contrasting them with what is involved in breaking them.

The commandment that will be the most difficult to discuss, especially with the younger students in the junior class, is the seventh one on adultery. Explain to them that "adultery" is having sexual relationships with someone other than his/her married mate. It is a sin adults and older teenagers become involved with sometimes. It involves a man and woman having sexual relationships, when one of them has another living husband or wife. Or a man or woman may be married and one or both of them become sexually active with other men or women. Children at this age have had enough exposure in sex education classes to understand what adultery is. This also provides an opportunity to teach them God's laws pertaining to sexuality.

That's it for now. Have a good class and you will with good preparation. Nothing can substitute for that. More "Tips" next week.

Notes

Lesson 7

Other Laws

One easy means of holding the attention of adults as well as children is to present or study something that is unusual or different. In this lesson, there are several laws that would seem very unusual to us today. In studying this lesson, pick out three or four of the laws that are unusual and have a discussion of these with the class. One of the laws is covered in today's lesson: the law concerning servants. You might also study those laws relating to the care and treatment of animals. Juniors are at the age to be especially concerned about them. A detailed discussion begins in Exodus 21:28; 22:1. Other information is found in 23:4, 5.

Another law different from any we are under today concerns borrowing and lending. A discussion of this is found in 22:25-27. No "interest" or "usury" was to be charged to the poor. If an item of security happened to be the person's cloak or raiment, it had to be returned before the evening. In the sight of God, things never were more important than people and their welfare. If you have access to *Clarke's Commentary* on this you will find some interesting sidelights to present to the class.

After you have dealt with some of the unusual laws, another interesting way to approach some of these laws is to show how they relate to some of the Ten Commandments. The students will have some of this to do in the student work for today, but it will be your job to show what more information is given in this section. You can have the students read or read to them yourself what is said about the Sabbath day in Exodus 20. Then read Exodus 23:10-12 and have the class pick out points not covered in Exodus 20.

In Exodus 22:1-4 a further discussion of "thou shalt not steal" is under consideration. Do the same with this you did with the Sabbath question above. Exodus 21:16 is a somewhat unusual way to discuss the topic of stealing. The penalty here is most severe. Have the class discuss the different penalties for stealing. Notice the severity of the crime and the severity of the penalty or punishment.

The subject of capital punishment enters the picture in today's lesson often. As a new approach when discussing this, pose a problem and apparent contradiction in the Scriptures and let the class discuss and wrestle with it for a minute or so. First, have someone read the sixth commandment, "Thou shalt not kill." Then have another student read Exodus 21:12 and another Exodus 21:15. These two Scriptures say under certain circumstances to "kill." Of course, the idea in the Ten Commandments is to each Jew, and as an individual he was forbidden to kill in the sense of "murder." When a person was guilty of certain crimes, it was demanded of the nation that this guilt be established with sufficient witnesses and then the guilty party was to be put to death for the crime.

Continue to see that each pupil keeps his grade correctly and since today's lesson involves a fraction you may have to help. Round off the grade to the next whole number if it is a fractional grade. More to come!

Lesson 8

The Tabernacle

Today's lesson will give you an opportunity to show how good you are at diagraming and drawing. Have your piece of chalk, a chalk board and a yard stick ready and you can have a lively and interesting class.

When you come to class, the students will already have studied the lesson on the tabernacle and you can make this class a real review for them by letting them do things they like. Have drawn on the board the tabernacle and the court as much to scale as possible. Have the pieces of furniture drawn in the tabernacle and in the courtyard and put numbers on nine things: the court, the most holy place, the holy place, the ark of the covenant, the altar of incense, the candlestick, the table, the laver, and the altar of burnt offerings. On the board beside your diagram write the above words and have a short line by each.

At the beginning of the class, tell the class you are going to have a game for them to play in connection with the lesson, if they will be good. If you have any discipline problem (and what teacher does not), this may help you for today. After going over the lesson and correcting their books, have different ones come to the board, take one numbered item, and match it with the proper word.

Another exercise you will find interesting is to figure out the sizes of the pieces of furniture in the tabernacle as well as the tabernacle itself. See that each student understands well what a cubit is. Then pick out some room or area all are familiar with and is about the size of the tabernacle. A 15 by 30 foot area is not large at all and that was the size of the tabernacle.

If you want to try another take one of the items in the tabernacle, such as the table for the shewbread (Exod. 37:10), and let the students figure out the size of this. It was only three feet long, 18 inches deep and 27 inches high. With the yard stick try to draw a table on the board with these dimensions. Or there may be a table in the room you can compare with the table of shewbread.

Another important point, not covered in the student book, but one they need to understand, is the interlude between Moses' two trips up the mountain. On the first trip and forty day stay, he received the law and instruction on the tabernacle and priesthood which we will study next time. When Moses returned, Aaron had built the golden calf and the people were worshipping it. After this was taken care of and the camp cleansed, Moses again ascended the mountain to receive the commandments on stone from God. You will remember that he had broken the first tables of stone. When he returned this second time, the tabernacle was constructed and on the first day of the first month of the second year it was set up by the command of God (Exod. 40:2, 17, 20). According to Exodus 19:1, the Israelites came to Sinai the third month. This would mean they had been camped at the foot of Sinai nine months. All of these facts will help the students see the historical

Notes

connection of various events they are familiar with: the golden calf, the giving of the tables of stone, the building of the tabernacle, and also show how long all this had taken.

If you have extra time, have the students tell you all they know about the purpose of the different things in the tabernacle and court. You will find a detailed discussion of these in Exodus 25-27 and 37-38. Know these chapters well.

Remember the value of review. Have some review of previous lessons planned each time.

Have a good class. Tips on teaching the priesthood and priestly office will be provided next time.

Lesson 9

The Priestly Office

In studying the Priesthood, you can divide the class into two periods of study with a study of the garments and appearance of the men first and then their work.

For a more complete definition of what some of the pieces were which the High Priest wore you may need to do some study in a Bible dictionary. Therefore, begin your study of this lesson early in the week. If you can find a good picture of what the High Priest looked like all dressed, take it to class and have the students identify some of the pieces of clothing (see *Zondervan's Pictorial Bible Dictionary*, 255 or search the internet).

More important in the lesson is the work God had given the high priest and other priests to do. Their work was equally as important as that of the prophets.

Offering of Sacrifices: More will be provided on this in the next lesson, so for the present there is no need to go into all the different kinds of sacrifices with all the details. You might be aware of the fact that there were daily sacrifices to be offered in the morning and evening, plus numerous others. These were for the priests themselves and for the people. The main point is that no one was authorized to offer sacrifices to God but the priests of the family of Aaron, of the tribe of Levi. Describe the kind of work involved with the selecting, killing, collecting of the blood, dressing, and offering the animals or birds as they were sometimes used.

It certainly was not a very pleasant job. All this was made necessary because people sinned and this was God's requirement because of sins. In all this, they were observing but a "shadow" (Heb. 10:1), "pattern" (Heb. 9:23), and "figure" (Heb. 9:24) of the real sacrifice, Christ. While talking about the work of sacrificing animals for sins, it will be the best time to make the comparison with Christ, our sacrifice today.

Representing the People: Find a good definition of a "mediator." This would be a clue word in studying this section. Again you can discuss here the two garments, the ephod and the breastplate, with the stones on which were written the names of the tribes.

You might use a modern illustration of how the government will sometimes send in a "federal mediator" to bring two sides together who are separated by certain differences. He is a person to go between and bring together. You might draw the diagram in the student text on the board and explain the different steps as you draw it in.

Teach the People: Everyone was responsible for knowing the Law of God. But it was the main responsibility of the priesthood to preserve the Law and teach it to the people. Read Deuteronomy 31:9-13. Here was a special time the priests were to read the Law to all the people. Because of their failure to teach this Law faithfully in future days, Israel

Notes

left God and was severely punished for it. The seventy year captivity in Babylon was due partly to the failure of the priests.

The priesthood of Aaron was intended to last until the coming of Christ and then it was to end.

Source Materials: *International Standard Bible Encyclopedia* is a good source for definitions. Many preachers will have it. Also *The New Smith's Bible Dictionary* is good but brief sometimes. Have a good class. More tips next time.

Lesson 10

Feast Days and Sacrifices

In teaching today's lesson, here are several specific suggestions for activities that are easy to plan and enjoyable for the students.

One is to drill on the meaning and purpose of each of the feasts. There was special significance attached to the observance of each of these Jewish feasts. Learn them well yourself and then here is an exercise you can have with your class. On the chalkboard plan three columns. Over the first one put "Time," which would be the month, day, and year. Over the second one put "Feast," and over the third put "Meaning." Let the students help you fill in the five feasts, their times of observance and meaning or significance. Drill them on these until they learn them well. After they learn them well, then you can erase the feasts and other facts under the column headings and write just one factor in, for example, "Passover." Then let some student give the time of observance and someone else the meaning. For another feast you might put 7th month, 1st day on the board, and they will give you the other information. Study Leviticus 23, Numbers 28, 29 and Deuteronomy 16. This will give you more information on these feasts.

To clarify some of the terms you will be reading, be on the lookout for these terms: "feast of weeks" which is the same as Pentecost. The "feast of unleavened bread" sometimes refers to the whole feast of the Passover and the following seven days of unleavened bread.

Another activity that will be of interest to the class is to clarify the calendar months as they correspond to ours. Only two would be necessary since the feasts came in the first and seventh months. Then Pentecost would be shortly after Passover, about fifty days after the time of Christ's death. Their first month, Abib, was in our March or April (corresponds to Easter) and our September or October would be at the time of their seventh month, Tishri.

When the class is familiar with all the feasts, then work on the memory verse for this reason. Three of these five feasts were to be accompanied by a journey of all the males to some designated place. Once they know the memory verse, they will know on which feast days they would make the trip. Two were only about fifty days apart in the first month. The other was the last in the seventh month.

Sometime during the period, ask the class if all these feasts lasted a week. Some did but some were only for one day. Have them learn which was for each period of time.

If time is left in the class, one more work project you might get several or even all the class to work on for a few minutes would be this: Have different ones figure how many animals of different kinds were sacrificed in just the daily sacrifices. How many in a year in the weekly sacrifices? Have others do this for the monthly sacrifices. I mentioned in their book that more animals were sacrificed at the feast of Taber-

Notes

nacles than at any other feast. Maybe that stirred their curiosity to want to know how many. In Numbers 29 you will find the answer by adding all the different sacrifices made each day. Then add the daily sacrifices for each day and for two days there were weekly sacrifices as well. The total is large.

With your own imaginative ideas and proper preparation you can have a good class. Work on it. Perhaps you will learn things you did not know yourself. Many are very unfamiliar with this part of the Bible. Have you had a good review lately? More next week.

Lesson 11

The Numbering of Israel

Getting students to participate in class is not always an easy thing to do. This is true especially if the class is more of a lecture presentation of the material than student participation. Therefore, work at preparing each class with things for the pupils to do during class. In this particular class you might add these activities to other things you have planned.

Help the class make a bar graph of the population of the tribes of Israel in the first census. That is the census discussed most in the lesson. They will likely remember the largest and smallest tribes best if the graph is prepared, not in the order in which they are presented in Numbers one, but start with the most populus tribe first and work down on a descending scale so the last tribes listed are the smallest. Here is an example of how you can do it.

Put this on the board during class and let them answer questions you ask as you go along. Example: What tribe is next? How high should I make this bar on the graph? Let different ones come to the board and help you.

Another interesting work project you can have is to show a comparison in the size of the tribes before the forty years in the wilderness and after. Numbers 26 will give you the details that you will have to prepare before class. You could have this done in columns beside one another: numbers for the "Census of Year Two" and "Census of Year Forty."

It is important to show in all this how the nation had its beginning in the first place and how it grew. Much of this material is in the text of the lesson. Make sure it is understood that all this is the result of the promise to Abraham as God was preparing the way for the coming of Christ through whom He would bless the world.

There is a big difference in seventy people and about 2,000,000 people. Some in the class may wonder how long it took. If the question comes up or if you have time for it otherwise, here is some helpful information:

- God promised Abraham a 400 year enslavement (Gen. 15:13). See also in connection with this Acts 7:6.

- It was to be in the fourth generation after the slavery began (Gen. 15:16). Exodus 6 gives this genealogy: Levi – Kohath – Amram – Moses and Aaron – Eleazar (and other sons of Aaron).

Today's memory verse is far from an exaggeration. Indeed they did grow rapidly.

Some of the students may want to take more time and work on these graphs at home on their own. If so, encourage them to make good ones in color and bring them to class next time. Post them on the board. These are just ideas for you to draw from if they can be of help. Have a good class. More next week.

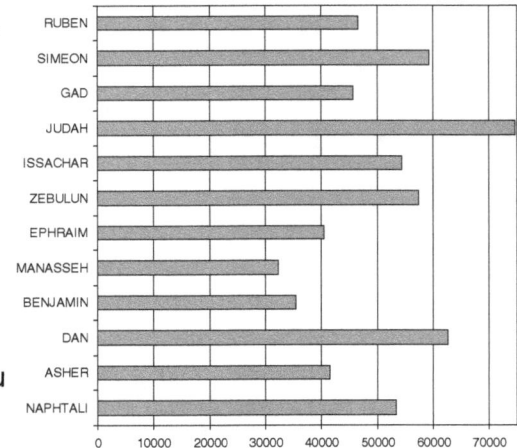

Notes

Living in the Desert

Numbers 11-19 contains the account of events in the Wilderness from Sinai to the end of the forty-year punishment. Perhaps you already are familiar with many of these stories, but review them and have several fresh in your mind to relate to the class.

In today's lesson only three were specificly referred to and, in this class, you should have plenty of material to give the class in addition to their written text. You might want to write an outline on the board of the events of this wandering.

(1) Murmuring at Taberah; (2) Lust at Kibroth-Hattaavah; Murmuring of Aaron and Miriam – Miriam's leprosy; (3) Spies' report and unbelieving Israel to stay forty years in the Wilderness; (4) Rebellion and death of Korah, Dothan, and Abiram.

Numbers 20 seems to be the beginning of their second attempt to go to Canaan and the events here and following are at the end of the forty years.

Get a good Bible dictionary and Baker's or Hurlbut's or Westminister's Bible atlas if possible and read up on the nature and characteristics of the wilderness. Have pictures if possible to show the class. Much information and many pictures are available on the internet.

Another thing you will do this time is continue the map work that was ended at Sinai in lesson 5. The places are not as easily located in the wilderness, so with the help of an atlas or dictionary, try to locate Kadesh-Barnea, sometimes called just "Kadesh," and spot it for the class. It will be in the northern part of the wilderness near Canaan. It is mentioned frequently and was probably the "headquarters" during the forty years. The next lesson will help the class complete the journey on their maps to the Jordan River on the East.

Perhaps more important than the stories of the wilderness wandering themselves is the reason why they were there in the first place. Discuss their discontentment and how today we can have the same sinful attitudes. 1 Corinthians 10:1-11 refers to this period of time in Israel's history and says these are examples teaching *us today* not to act as they acted. Read also, in preparation, Jude 16 and Philippians 2:14. Also helpful will be I Timothy 6:6-8 and Philippians 4:11-14 on the subject of "contentment."

The other major problem was disbelief and is really or can be a cause of murmuring. This is the specific term used in Hebrews 3:19. God had said that He would be with them and they could take the land. They did not believe that. They did not understand how an invisible God could help them and evidently thought it would be all on their own power. When they tried to conquer Canaan, God showed them they could not do it without His help.

With map work, various interesting stories, a description of the wilderness, pictures, and a discussion of the two main reasons for all their troubles, you will have a busy class with lots to do this time.

Teachers "complain" sometimes that they just do not have enough material to keep them busy the whole class. I trust that has not been a problem to you. When a teacher prepares well ahead of time and uses imagination in getting the students to do things relating to the class study there will be no problem. I hope you enjoy teaching these last two lessons. A final tip next time.

Notes

A teacher always has to ask a personal question: "How is the best way I can use my time?" In this final lesson, I would suggest it be divided into two segments. The first relates to today's lesson. Cover the material with the class and let two or three tell the story of the death of Moses. Let two or three others tell why Moses was not allowed to enter Canaan and give the story. Read carefully Numbers 20. We have often heard that the reason Moses did not enter Canaan was because he struck the rock. That, however, is not the reason God gave him. The trouble was really twofold. He did strike the rock, but *what he said* was what God emphasized in his punishment. In fact, God did not even refer to the striking of the rock. The real sin here was the failure of Moses to give God the glory for the miracle and provision of water. Make sure the class understands the real sin of Moses (see Ps. 106:32-33).

Go over the book and check the material and answers of the students. Then spend the rest of the time in review of the whole 13 week period.

There is nothing like review to reinforce memory and learning. As was suggested at the first of the quarter, review every week or two is the best way review can be handled. But at the end of a study like this "tie together" the story and make it one story instead of thirteen.

You have two ways available through which to review. One is the map study. Help them finish that today, showing their journey down and around the land of Edom then up the eastern side of the country and Dead Sea. They fought and defeated the countries all up and down the east of the Jordan River as a Bible atlas will show. They came to Nebo and the Plains of Moab for the final days of Moses with Israel. Review by using the map they have prepared in their book (p. 56).

Another way to review is to ask questions and have them tell stories you have studied. Select several good questions from each lesson so as to tie the whole story together. The class might be asked to give several events in the first forty years of the life of Moses. Then ask for events in the other two forty year periods. There were two major events at Sinai: the giving of the law and the building of the tabernacle. Think of the good review you can have on the feasts and sacrifices and the numbering of the Israelites. When you have once covered the material then drill, drill, drill; review, review, review.

Every teacher has his or her own personality and manner of teaching. It is therefore, out of place for one teacher to try to get another teacher to fit his mold. What we have been trying to do in the "Tips" is make some suggestions that have proven helpful in the past in getting pupils to learn. But along with learning, try to get them to enjoy learning the Bible. If some of these suggestions in class procedure and suggestions for teaching have proved helpful, the time spent in preparation of this has been adequately rewarded.

From one teacher to another: My thanks to you for having me in to take this part in your class.

Lesson 1

Faith That Moves

The Lesson Plan: This lesson is designed to show how real faith will always move the person who has it to obey the law of God. This is a very important principle of righteousness. The child must be made to feel the urgency of immediate action when God speaks. Instill in the child's mind that he can stand against one or a thousand when he stands with God. Keep this thread of thought before the student.

Scripture Texts: The basic scripture texts for this lesson include, Genesis 5:28-6:22; Hebrews 11; and 1 Peter 3:18-21. Individual passages will be noted separately in the lesson when the reference is not included in the above passages. Be familiar with every scripture reference in the child's workbook. The teacher should prepare the lesson in the book and know the lesson well. The child will get much more out of a lesson the teacher has prepared well and knows.

Guidelines: Memorize the memory verse. Background material for the memory verse can be found in Genesis 6. The *World Book Dictionary's* definition of "faith" is "a belief without proof." Bible "faith" is a firm conviction based on evidence. What evidences do we have for belief in God?

I. Noah: A Man of Faith

Show in this section that the majority are seldom, if ever, right in religion. Make the child feel secure with God and insecure with the multitudes who may refuse to do His will. Passages which may help get this thought across in your own words may include Exodus 23:2; Matthew 7:13-14; Romans 3:4. Make the child feel that finding grace in the eyes of the Lord is greater than all the world can offer.

II. Noah's Faith Moved Him to Obey God

God is displeased with people who are always thinking evil thoughts and who tell dirty stories and listen to the same. There is both time and place for a good funny story but not for bad stories and foolish talk (Eph. 5:4). Instead of making up evil things, Noah used his time to move in obedience to God. The world may laugh at you for doing right but they will respect you nevertheless (1 Pet. 2:11-12). We can preach the best sermons by doing what the Lord says.

III. How Faith Moves Us Today

Compare the warnings that God has given us to those He gave the people in the days of Noah. The fire that one day will destroy the world is just as sure as the flood that has already taken place. We must always be as ready as Noah.

IV. Be on the Lord's Side

Describe the happiness that we will have on that day when we shall have done the will of the Lord. It might be well here to show both happiness and fear as motives for obedience (Rom. 8:18; 11:22; 2 Cor. 4:17; Heb. 10:31). It is far better to be with the few who are saved than the multitudes who will be lost! The Lord knows our thoughts.

V. A Tip for the Teacher

A good time to begin preparation for your next week's class is right after you teach this class. Alone, you can analyze both yourself and your class and the material will still be fresh on your mind. The influence you may have on one of your students cannot be overestimated. You cannot prepare too much.

Answers to Questions

Exercise 1. Match the Following: Hebrews 11

1. c. Offered (v. 21)
2. f. Moved with fear (v. 7)
3. d. Obeyed, sojourned (vv. 8-9)
4. g. Made mention (v. 22)
5. a. Blessed (v. 21)
6. i. Refused, was hid (vv. 23-24)
7. b. Perished not (v. 31)
8. j. Received strength (v. 11)
9. e. Fell down (v. 30)
10. h. Passed through the Red Sea (v. 29)

Exercise 2. Fill in the Blanks

1. preacher, righteousness (2 Pet. 2:5)
2. eight souls, water (1 Pet. 3:20)
3. baptism (1 Pet. 3:21)
4. faith, sight (2 Cor. 5:7)
5. Comfort (Gen. 5:29)
6. wickedness, intent, thoughts, evil (Gen. 6:5)
7. 120 (Gen. 6:3)
8. all, commanded (Gen. 6:22)
9. grace (Gen. 6:8)
10. bow, flood (Gen. 9:13)

Exercise 3. True and False

1. True (Acts 5:29)
2. False (1 Pet. 3:21)
3. False (Gen. 6:3; 1 Pet. 3:18-20; 2 Pet. 2:5)
4. True (2 Pet. 2:5; 1 Pet. 3:20, while ark was preparing)
5. False (Gen. 6:5-6)

Exercise 4. For Class Discussion:

When Noah obeyed God, his very life stood in condemnation to all who had disobeyed Him. Every time an evil man looked at Noah, he could be reminded of God's condemnation of his life. When a person today obeys the gospel, lives the gospel, and preaches the gospel, his life shines as a constant reminder of God's wrath upon all who have failed to obey the gospel. Hereby, the world stands condemned.

Every command of God has a two-fold effect upon all mankind. For those who obey His commands, the commands will be a witness for his forgiveness. For those who disobey, the command becomes a witness and reason for destruction. Give any illustrations of your own to illustrate these principles of righteousness.

Notes

Notes

The Lesson Plan: This lesson is designed to create in the child an unfaltering trust in the Lord. A firm belief in the justice and power of God is an essential principle of righteousness. The child must be made to feel complete confidence in the precious promises of God. This confidence will beget a secure feeling during times of trial and temptation. Instill in the student the confidence that God will never betray our trust in Him. Show how God's promises to us today, as with Abraham, are always conditional upon our faithfulness and trust in Him.

Scripture Texts: The scripture texts for this lesson are chosen to give the student a complete picture of Abraham who trusted in God. They include: Genesis 12:1-5; 22:1-18; Romans 4:16-25; Hebrews 11:8-10, 17-19; and James 2:21-24. Other passages will be listed separately in the text. Be familiar with every scripture in the workbook. Prepare well your lesson. The success of this lesson depends largely upon the preparation and presentation of you the teacher.

Guidelines: Memorize the memory verse and emphasize its meaning throughout the lesson. "Trust" is defined by the *World Book Dictionary*. The word "sustain" is also defined, "to keep up; to keep going." Give illustrations of your own to emphasize this point. Remember always to use language that is common both to you and the student. Use familiar words and simple sentences, and speak to be heard and understood. Encourage each student to study at least two hours on each lesson at home. Thus, greater good will be derived.

I. Abraham Trusted in the Lord

Emphasize in this section how each individual must learn to trust in the Lord with all his heart. Explain how God has called each of us from a world of sin to a home in heaven when we die. As Abraham was willing to leave his home and country to journey toward Canaan land, so we must be willing to forsake all things in this life to reach heaven after awhile (Matt. 19:29-30). Abraham did not understand exactly where he was going but he kept moving and trusted God to lead him. We cannot see heaven with our physical eye but, if we trust and obey, the Lord will lead us in the light of His word to a home in glory in the sweet by and by.

II. Abraham Firmly Trusted God's Promise

Emphasize to the student that it is impossible for God to lie (Heb. 6:18), and that nothing is impossible for Him to do. Our failure to understand how God does what He does is no reason to distrust Him. Show how God's ways are higher than our ways and His thoughts than our thoughts (Isa. 55:8-9). We must guard against trying to limit what God can do by our inability to understand. This is why we trust Him.

III. Abraham Trusted God When He Was Tempted

Show how God has promised not to allow us to be tempted above what we are able to bear (1 Cor. 10:13). The only defense we have against temptation is the word of God (Eph. 6:13-16). Emphasize the importance of studying God's word that we may know His will when temptation comes our way. If we know God's will and trust in Him with all our hearts, we will always do what is right (cf., 2 Tim. 2:15).

IV. Faith Made Perfect Through Obedience

Explain why Abraham was not justified by faith only. Show how the scripture (Gen. 15:6) was fulfilled and Abraham's faith made perfect (seven chapters later—Gen. 22:12) only after Abraham had obeyed God. Likewise, our faith is made perfect only after we trust in the Lord and do His will.

Exercise 1. Match the Following: Note To Teacher: Show the student how to use the center-column reference to learn the meaning of words numbered in the text. E.g. perfect, Abraham, and Jehovah-jireh (Gen. 17:1, 5; 22:14).

1. g (Gen. 17:1)
2. j (Jas. 2:23)
3. e (Gen. 22:12)
4. a (Gen. 22:14)
5. c (Heb. 11:17)
6. i (Rom. 4:21)
7. d (Heb. 11:10)
8. f (Rom. 4:18)
9. h (Gen. 17:5)
10. b (Heb. 11:12)

Exercise 2. Fill in the Blanks:
1. city, foundations, builder, maker (Heb. 11:10)
2. Mesopotamia, Haran (Acts 7:2)
3. Abram's, Abraham, father, nations (Gen. 17:7)
4. seed, obeyed, voice (Gen. 22:18)
5. Christ's, seed, heirs, promise (Gal. 3:29)
6. 75, Haran (Gen. 12:4)
7. Abram, shield, great reward (Gen. 15:1)
8. The Lord will provide (KJV: Jehovah-jireh), provide (Gen. 22:14)
9. Righteousness, friend (James 2:23)

Exercise 3. True And False:
1. True (Gen. 12:4) Note to teacher: Show how Rom. 4:20 supports the definition of trust.
2. False (Rom. 4:20)
3. False (Gen. 11:32)
4. True (Gen. 22:13; James 2:23)

Exercise 4. For Class Discussion:

Show how God had reference to all people being blessed in Christ Jesus. The promise to Abraham was fulfilled in Christ. When a person is baptized into Christ, he becomes an heir of the blessings God promised to Abraham.

Notes

Lesson 3

Patience That Endures

The Lesson Plan: One of the most important principles of righteousness, and about the hardest to learn at any age, is patience. To ensure a fruitful life in the kingdom of God, it is imperative that every young person learn this lesson early and learn it well. Impress upon the child's mind that God will always do what is best for His children. Every commandment can be obeyed, every problem can be solved, every requirement can be met, and every blessing can be enjoyed – with patience! Though we may not have the patience of Job, we do have the same God as Job who will not allow us to be tempted above what we are able to bear, but will care for us and watch over us in our hour of trouble and trial. Emphasize this thought throughout the lesson.

Scripture Texts: The scripture texts selected for this lesson show the end result of patience. They include: Job 1; 2; 42:12-17; Romans 5:3-5; Hebrews 10:32-36; 12:1-2; James 1:3-4, 12; 5:7-11. References to additional scriptures will appear in the workbook. Careful preparation of each lesson is very important. Show enthusiasm in your class. Make each child feel his need for learning patience.

Guidelines: Memorize the memory verse and emphasize again that the end of a thing is better than the beginning (Eccl. 7:8). "Patience" and "endurance" are both defined by *World Book Dictionary*. Give illustrations of your own, showing patience at work in our everyday lives. For example, we show patience when we learn not to hold a grudge against another (Jas. 5:9). Encourage each child to study the lesson thoroughly and to read it over several times before class.

I. Job Patiently Endures

Emphasize the danger here of loving material possessions more than God. The fashions of this world will pass away (1 Cor. 7:31) but God will abide forever. We must guard against any attachment to this life that may cause us to become bitter against God when we suffer a loss. We, as Job, must love the truth for the truth's sake (2 John 1-2). We must love to do right because it is always right to do right and always wrong to do wrong. We should want to serve God because He is God and not for any consideration of reward. Try to get this concept across to the class.

II. Job Endures Even Greater Losses

Job lost his property, family and loved ones, his health, and even his good reputation among his friends. Yet, his love and devotion to God were greater than any of these. In all this, Job showed great patience. We must try to imitate his example. We may feel we cannot endure our grief but we can and will, if we exercise patience and wait it out. Show that we must live godly lives and trust in the Lord with all our heart if we are to hold out unto the end as Job did (cf. 2 Tim. 3:10-12).

III. The End Is Better Than the Beginning

Emphasize here the importance of end thinking. You may use the strait and wide gates to illustrate your point (Matt. 7:13-14). Looking from this end, the strait gate has no appeal. Looking back from eternity, it is beautiful and the reward is great! Show how the sufferings of this life are not worthy to be compared to the glory that shall be revealed hereafter (Rom. 8:18).

IV. Lesson To Learn

God will withhold no good thing from any of His children. We should be willing to endure anything which makes us better. Medicine may taste bad but it may be the best thing for our physical bodies. Trials are bitter and hard to take while upon us but they will make us stronger spiritually and will teach us patience.

V. A Tip for the Teacher

Christ is the Master teacher. He continually taught new concepts to His disciples by using concepts familiar to them all. We, as Christ, must first determine what concepts are familiar to our listeners, then bridge the gap between the known and the unknown.

Answers in Lesson 3
Exercise 1. Fill in the Blanks

1. Weary, season, reap, heart (Gal. 6:9)
2. Aforetime, learning, comfort, hope (Rom. 15:4)
3. Skin, life (Job 2:4)
4. Money, root, faith, patience (1 Tim. 6:10-11)
5. Steadfast, unmovable, Lord, labor, vain (1 Cor. 15:58)
6. Sluggish, faith, patience (Heb. 6:12)
7. Blameless, upright, fears, shuns (Job 1:8)

Exercise 2. True and False

1. False (Eccl. 7:8)
2. True (Rom. 15:4)
3. False (Heb. 10:32)
4. True (Job 1:6)
5. True (Job 42:7)

Exercise 3. For Class Discussion

Emphasize how the devil as a roaring lion is out to get us (1 Pet. 5:8). Christ is the only one who has successfully overcome him. Our only hope in overcoming Satan is with the help of Christ. Salvation to all men could not be offered until Christ shed His blood on Calvary. Scriptures helpful in portraying this beautiful picture are as follows: Luke 11:21-22; Romans 3:23-26; Hebrews 2:14-15; Revelation 12:10-11. You might tell how Christ waited patiently while He was disowned, dishonored, and forsaken until He died on the cross.

Many times the Christian's life is compared to a race (cf. 1 Cor. 9:24-25; 2 Tim. 2:5; Heb. 12:1-2). Explain how exercise makes our bodies healthy and strong. In like manner, trials make our faith stronger. The more we exercise, the stronger we become. The more we undergo trials, the stronger and more patient we become.

Notes

Lesson 4

Respect for Authority

The Lesson Plan: God places more emphasis upon obedience and respect for His authority than for all the sacrifices that man can offer (1 Sam. 15:22). If we have the proper attitude, we will always have respect for the authority of God and will obey His will in every relationship in life. The aim of this lesson is to instill in each child a thankfulness and appreciation for authority and to show how respect for authority is the foundation of everything we do in this life that is right. It is the only way truly to be free. Show in this present age how men who seek freedom from all law and authority always end up in bondage. Those who seek freedom from the law become themselves slaves to whatever sin they may follow (John 8:33-34; Rom. 6:16; 2 Pet. 2:19). Every guilty soul in prison is there because he failed somewhere along the way to respect authority. Stress this!

Scripture Texts: The scripture texts show both the good consequences for showing respect for authority and the bad consequences for showing disrespect. The main texts are Numbers 16; Ephesians 6:1-3; Romans 13:1-4. Other scripture that will be helpful in preparation for this lesson will appear elsewhere throughout the workbook. Throughout the lesson, show how our respect for authority must be absolute and not just half-hearted. One either respects authority or he does not. It just takes one small hole in a tire to let all the air out. Likewise, it takes just one act of disrespect for authority to start us on the road to destruction.

Guidelines: Memorize the memory verse and show how in every way our attitude must always be directed towards the commandments of God. Get on the level with the children. Sympathize with their feelings but always hold up the goal of truth and righteousness. Assure them that they will never be ashamed when they allow the word of God to direct their every course in life (Rom. 5:3-5; 1 Pet. 4:11, 16).

I. Korah Shows Disrespect for the Authority of God

Show how Korah could have been a faithful worker in the Tabernacle had he respected God's authority and selection of Moses and Aaron. Explain that the way up in life as well as in the kingdom of God is not by pulling somebody else down. When we humble ourselves before God and one another, we will rise to the top (Luke 14:11). God does not approve of self-appointed leaders in His kingdom (2 Cor. 10:18; 3 John 9-10). God will always punish those who refuse to submit to His authority. Christ is the prophet like unto Moses before whom we all must submit (Deut. 18:15,18-19; Acts 3:22-23).

II. We Show Respect for Authority by Obeying Our Parents

To honor thy father and mother is the first commandment with promise (Exod. 20:12). The attitude of thankfulness and appreciation that comes from honoring our parents will grow and be useful in making right choices throughout life. By so doing, it will be well with us in every walk of life and our years upon this earth should be increased. Godliness with contentment is always great gain (1 Tim. 6:6). Point out that our parents who brought us into this world and cared for us when we were sick and helpless know best what is good for us in this life. We should listen carefully when our parents teach us and show respect always for their authority.

III. We Show Respect for the Authority of God by Obeying the Laws of the Land.

Stress again the importance of having the right attitude and respect for authority in general. As the teacher, you will not have to elaborate upon particular violations of law if you can get the student to see the big picture of what respect for authority really is. If the attitude of heart is right, our every deed will have the favor both of God and man.

IV. Tips for the Teacher

Give thorough preparation to this very important principle of righteousness. Examine your own heart and make sure you have the proper respect for the authority of God. Pray to the Lord for wisdom to be able to impress upon the minds of your students the whole of man—to fear God and to keep His commandments (Eccl. 12:13). The influence you may have in this lesson may mean the difference in the salvation or damnation of some child present. Use illustrations in your own life or in life that is lived around you to emphasize the consequences both good and bad of showing respect or disrespect for the authority of God.

Answers in Lesson 4
Exercise 1. Complete The Puzzle:
The name under the star is C-H-R-I-S-T, written from top to bottom.

1. Censer
2. Korah
3. Abiram
4. Levites
5. Moses
6. Dathan

Exercise 2. Fill in the Blanks:
1. obey, honor (Eph. 6:1-2)
2. instruction, forsake, law (Prov. 1:8)
3. fire, consumed, 250 (Num. 16:35)
4. censers, covering, memorial (Num. 16:39-40)
5. ministers, good, avenger, wrath (Rom. 13:3-4)
6. resists, ordinance (Rom. 13:3)

Exercise 3. For Class Discussion:
Explain how parents with more experience can see farther down the road of life than their children. Parents correct children when they see them going in the direction of harm or destruction. Illustrate your point by explaining how a parent might punish a child for running into a busy street to play. The child is unaware of the tremendous danger of the traffic that can cripple or kill him. The parent is aware and does not want the child harmed. Have the children to give illustrations of their own.

Notes

Lesson 5

Reverence for God's Will in Religion

The Lesson Plan: "It is with men as with wheat; the light heads are erect even in the presence of Omnipotence, but the full heads bow in reverence before Him" (Cooke). "The fear of the Lord is the beginning of wisdom. . ." (Prov. 9:10).

The more we learn about God, the deeper our appreciation and respect will be for Him. Emphasize this fact throughout the lesson. The truly great men of the Bible always stood in wonder and awe at the greatness of God. Even Jesus, out of deep respect for His Father, fell on His face when He prayed to Him (Matt. 26:39).

A passage like Amos 5:13 may help you with a description of God's greatness to the class. The very thought of standing before our God, who is so great, should help us to have and to show a deep reverence for His will. Emphasize throughout the lesson the deep respect we are to have for the word of God. When the Bible is read, we must remain silent and listen because the God of heaven and earth is speaking.

Scripture Texts: The scripture texts selected for this lesson show examples of irreverence for the will of God in contrast to what sincere reverence should be. The two examples illustrate vividly the exactness with which we must carry out the will of God. There can be no deep respect for God if we are unwilling to do exactly as He has commanded. The main texts are: Deuteronomy 10:1-5; 31:24-27; Hebrews 9:1-5; 2 Samuel 6:1-8 and Leviticus 10:1-3. Emphasize throughout the lesson that our attitude today towards God's will must be the same attitude Christ displayed towards His Father's will when He said, "For I came down from heaven, not to do My own will, but the will of Him that sent Me" (John 6:38).

Guidelines: Memorize the memory verse and point out how the Lord has promised to hold us up that we might be safe if we have respect for His will (Matt. 28:20; Rom. 8:28, 31; 1 Cor. 10:13; Heb. 13:5). Emphasize how God's children have everything to gain and nothing to lose when they put Him first and show reverence for His will. One the other hand, show how we have nothing to gain and everything to lose when we do not respect His will. "Reverence" is defined from *World Book Dictionary*.

I. David and Uzzah Fail to Reverence God's Will

Read Exodus 25:10-22 to familiarize yourself with a complete description of the ark's construction. Hebrews 9:4 lists the full contents of the ark, except for the book of the law mentioned in Deuteronomy 31:24-27. Use the example of David's new cart to drive home the point that God's plan cannot be improved upon. Had the men borne the ark upon their shoulders like God said, there would have been no oxen to stumble. Point out today that, when people change the Lord's plan for the work and worship of His church, they will always be doomed to failure. Use the example of Uzzah to emphasize the fact that good intentions are never a substitute for doing exactly what God has said.

It would have been better for the ark to have been shaken and to have fallen off the cart than for Uzzah to have touched it and died.

II. Nadab and Abihu Offered Strange Fire

In the example of Nadab and Abihu, you may again emphasize the point that God says what He means and means what He says. Point out that, when we learn to show reverence for God's will in small things the big things will take care of themselves. God has graciously made known His will unto us and we all must show a deep respect for God and His will by doing exactly as He says in all things.

III. Tips for the Teacher

Put feeling with your facts as you endeavor to teach your children. Some pupils have bright minds but hard hearts. Others have soft hearts but weakened intellects. Try to determine which is the case with each child and appeal to them accordingly and individually so you can win them. This lesson on reverence calls upon the innermost feelings of the heart together with truth that is to be applied. If you will help your students to have reverence towards God's will, you must put these two together in your teaching. Create an atmosphere of deep respect mixed with wonder, awe, and love in your class room. Do not be afraid to be enthusiastic in your presentation.

Answers in Lesson 5
Exercise 1. True and False
1. False (shittim wood, Exod. 25:10)
2. True (Lev. 16:12)
3. False (2 Sam. 6:3)
4. True (Deut. 10:4)
5. False (Heb. 9:4)

Exercise 2. Match the Following
1. d (Deut. 10:2)
2. e (Exod. 25:15)
3. f (2 Sam. 6:6)
4. a (Deut. 10:2)
5. h (Exod. 25:10; Deut. 10:1)
6. i. (1 Chron. 24:1-2)
7. b (Exod. 25:14)
8. j (Matt. 7:21)
9. g (2 Sam. 6:6)
10. c (Lev. 16:2)

Exercise 3. For Class Discussion

Man does not help God. Neither does God need our help. God only wants our deep respect for His will. He is pleased when we show our deep respect by doing His will.

We must pay close attention to what God has said. If what we are doing is not included in what God has said, then it is wrong. God commanded Moses to build an ark of shittim wood. He did not forbid the use of cedar wood, but we know it would have been wrong. Why? Simply because cedar and shittim are different kinds of wood and God said shittim wood.

Notes

Lesson 6
Courage to Stand

The Lesson Plan: This lesson is designed to show courage as a principle of righteousness dependent upon one's complete adherence to Jehovah God and His word. The child should be made to feel the need of showing courage in doing the will of God wherever he may be or whatever may be the cost.

Scripture Texts: The basic scripture texts for this lesson include, Numbers 14; I Samuel 17; I Kings 18; and Acts 5. The teacher should be familiar with every scripture reference in the child's workbook. The teacher should prepare the lesson in the workbook. Study well your lesson that you may know well that which you would teach the children.

Guidelines: Memorize the memory verse and learn the historical background of the verse by studying the context (Deut. 31:1-6). This verse can serve as the thread of thought throughout the lesson.

The definition of "courage" is taken from the *World Book Dictionary*. Though time will not allow every scripture to be used, the teacher should endeavor to direct the study to follow at least the general thought in the lesson plan.

I. A Courageous Servant Becomes a Leader
Show how a servant learns to be courageous first of all in small things. Joshua learned to be a faithful servant before he could be a faithful leader (Exod. 24:13). He was faithful as a young man and the Lord used him for even greater work when he was older. Show how God will use us today in His work if we will prepare ourselves (Phil. 2:12-13). Show the importance of obeying God while young (Eccl. 12:1), that we might be better prepared to be used by the Lord when we are older. Show in each example in the lesson how the servant of the Lord always looked to God for strength and did not rely upon himself. You might emphasize Psalm 73:26.

II. A Shepherd Boy with an Unfailing Heart
If we are on the Lord's side, no matter how great the opposition, the servant of the Lord will always win. God and His word are stronger than swords and spears to fight evil (1 Sam. 17:44-45; 2 Cor. 10:4; Eph. 6:10-18). If we trust in the Lord as we study and obey His word, we will never fear any man, not even the devil himself (1 Pet. 3:13-14). Show how sin will cause a man to lose his strength (Psa. 31:10). Tell how God will ultimately punish all the enemies of His children (Josh. 10:25), and how the courageous servant of the Lord will always prosper if he continues to do the Lord's will (Josh. 22:13).

III. Elijah Stands Alone Against 450 Men
Emphasize how the servant of the Lord must, not only show courage in keeping the commandments of God, but also in opposing false teachers and false worship. Show also that the servant must have the right attitude at all times and preach the truth with love (Eph. 4:15). We

must first make sure we are right and then have the courage to stand even against rulers and preach unto them the will of the Lord.

IV. Obey God Rather Than Man

Show here that people who do not love the Lord cannot bear to have their sins pointed out. This is the reason the Jews hated Jesus and crucified Him (John 7:7). Sinful people today will often make fun of a Christian and say ugly and hurtful things to and about him (1 Pet. 3:15-16). Yet, the Lord is pleased with those who have the courage to suffer for His name's sake (1 Pet. 2:19-20; 3:17-18). It takes real courage to stand for the truth and do what is right.

V. The Teacher's Encouragement

Yours is the greatest work on earth, that of forming in young minds the principles of righteousness and indelible impressions which will influence the lives of your students in the days ahead. Equip yourselves well for the responsible task you have undertaken. Your influence as a teacher will save many souls.

Answers in Lesson 6 (Don't demand that the students have these exact words.)

1. That he be strong and courageous and observe to do according to all the law which Moses commanded (vv. 7-8).

2. Christ has promised to be with and never forsake those who teach His word and remain faithful.

3. He fought a lion and a bear who took one of the sheep out of the flock. The Lord delivered him.

4. He had not proved it. David had the Lord on his side.

5. Quit halting between two opinions (limping between two sides, ASV). To choose either God or Baal because they could not serve both. No.

6. A contest between his God, Jehovah, and their god, Baal.

7. Yes, we are commanded to question them. They will get mad many times and may react violently.

8. They rejoiced that they were counted worthy to suffer shame for the name of Christ. They kept on preaching.

9. They should not fear or be afraid of any man. A person who suffers for righteousness' sake should be happy.

10. No. The flesh is weak and will fail. Only God can supply sufficient strength to stand.

For Class Discussion

Show how God's Word has a two-fold power. It can overcome giants of sin and has also the power to save our souls eternally. Note that every piece of armor listed in the Ephesian passage has some reference to the Word.

Relate some incident in the news or in the town where you live that illustrates courage. Show how much greater it is to show courage for God which has eternal reward. Use any other Bible characters to illustrate courage in light of the lesson you have studied. Be familiar with the characters referred to in Hebrews 11:32-38.

Notes

Necessity of Complete Obedience in Glorifying God

The Lesson Plan: "It ought to be the great care of every one of us to follow the Lord fully. We must follow Him uprightly, without dissembling; cheerfully, without disputing; and constantly, without declining" (Matthew Henry). The aim of this lesson is to instill in each child an awareness of the supreme importance of complete obedience to God. When we fail to submit our total self and will unto God, we rob Him of His glory and are guilty of disobedience. Complete obedience unto God will cure us of the dangerous habit of boasting about our own accomplishments.

God does not want us to boast about what we do in this life. When we boast about what we have done, we rob God of His glory. For example, God calls all men into His service through obedience to the gospel (2 Thess. 2:14). If the gospel could be understood only by a wise man, then he would be tempted to glory more in his wisdom than in the living God. Therefore, God has chosen very simple things for us to do so a wise person cannot glory in his wisdom. Also, God has chosen the weak things to shame those who would glory in their strength. He has chosen the base and simple everyday things to put to shame those who would glory in their riches (1 Cor. 1:26-31). This way, man can only give glory to God for what he does and has nothing left to glory in himself.

Scripture Texts: The scripture texts tell of Saul, Naaman, and Joshua. We find in these men examples of disobedience, delayed obedience, and complete obedience. The principle texts are: 1 Samuel 15:1-23; 2 Kings 5:1-16; Joshua 6:1-6. The reference to 1 Corinthians 1:26-31 is for the purpose of giving emphasis to the lesson. Drive home the principle of complete obedience as a permanent standard of life by which all our relationships to God must be measured. If this principle is not firmly established in the child's mind, all the facts you can teach the child will be to no avail. Inspire your students to want to obey God by complete obedience to Him.

Guidelines: Memorize the memory verse and emphasize how our every thought is to be centered upon obedience to Christ. Explain to the child how we exalt ourselves and others above the knowledge of God when we insist on doing what we or others think instead of what God says. By exalting ourselves above the knowledge of God, we rob Him of His glory. Motivate the child to action on this point. Remember that the motivations and principles you establish in the hearts of your students today will remain there and will be their guides in making right decisions tomorrow.

I. Saul Falls Short of Complete Obedience

Show how Saul had a humble beginning, was bashful, and was little in his own sight (1 Sam. 10:22-23; 15:17). But after he became king he began to think more highly of himself than he should have and that is when he stopped glorifying God through complete obedience. He even tried to convince Samuel that he had obeyed the voice of the Lord (15:20), but Samuel knew that he had not. Our obedience must be from our whole heart or not at all (Rom. 6:17-18). God will not accept our worship unto Him if we do not obey Him completely in everything. Obedience from the heart is better than sacrifices that we may offer the Lord. Emphasize this principle throughout the lesson.

II. Naaman Glorifies God When He Obeyed Him Completely

Show in the story of Naaman how the memory verse applies. Also, illustrate the principle found in 1 Corinthians 1:26-31. God, as it were, stripped off the captain's bars from Naaman together with all his mighty valor, worldly greatness, and honor. Naaman was truly humbled before God and could not boast, when he returned home, of anything he had done. When he came up out of the water, he glorified God and was thankful. When we come up out of the watery grave of baptism, we have nothing about which to boast. Like Naaman of old, we can merely glorify God and be truly thankful (Rom. 6:17-18).

III. By Complete Obedience the Walls of Jericho Fell

Relate this story with enthusiasm. Show the excitement that must have grown in the hearts of God's children as they marched around the walls daily and especially as they marched for the seventh time on the seventh day. Tell of the good feeling that we will always have when we know we have done exactly what God has said. You may illustrate this same feeling of excitement when we do exactly as our parents have asked us to do. Things will always turn out well in life when we give glory to God and do as we are told.

IV. Tips for the Teacher:

Remember as a teacher of God's word, you are interested, not only in improving the child's intellect, but in developing his will and sensitivities as well. Concentrate upon putting heart and feeling into your teaching. Motivate the child with love as well as Bible facts.

Answers in Lesson 7
Exercise 1. Multiple Choice:
1. continually each day and a long blast after the seventh time on the last day (Josh. 6:5, 8-9, 13).
2. was between two groups of armed men (Josh. 6:13).
3. he glorified the God of all the earth (2 Kings 5:15)
4. to obey the prophet who said to wash and be clean (2 Kings 5:13).
5. they had attacked Israel when they first came out of Egypt (1 Sam. 15:2).
6. is better than sacrifices (1 Sam. 15:22).

Exercise 2. Fill in the Blanks:
1. Jericho, severely, children, Israel (Josh. 6:1).
2. priests, war, ram's horns (Josh. 6:3-4).
3. great, honorable, Syrian, leper (2 Kings 5:1).
4. Rebellion, witchcraft, stubborness, iniquity, idolatry (1 Sam. 15:23).
5. people, feared (1 Sam. 15:24).

Notes

The Lesson Plan: A worship scene in heaven is described by all who fell on their faces before the throne, and worshipped God, saying, ". . . Blessing, and glory, and wisdom, and thanksgiving, and honor, and power, and might, be unto our God for ever and ever. Amen" (Rev. 7:12). The aim of this lesson is to impress indelibly upon the younger minds the absolute importance of faithful worship to Jehovah God. To be faithful, you might suggest, is like keeping a promise. When we worship and serve God faithfully, we are keeping our promise to love Him with all our hearts. God in turn will keep His promise to save us in heaven after this life is over. Emphasize the fact that worship to God must never be thought of as a dreadful duty but as a blessed privilege. Show the importance of worshipping God with all the heart by having our minds concentrated upon everything we do in worship. We must avoid always the danger of holding to certain forms while denying the power thereof (2 Tim. 3:5).

Scripture Texts: The scripture texts selected for this lesson illustrate the character and attitude of Daniel and the parents of Jesus in their faithful worship to God. The main texts are: Daniel 1:1-8; 6:1-24; Luke 2:40-45. Other scriptures pertinent to the subject at hand will appear elsewhere in the text. Since it is so easy sometimes to take our worship to God for granted, careful preparation must be given to this most important lesson. The child must be made to feel a deep need and desire to worship God.

Be an example to the children. Do not be afraid to put feeling into your teaching. The children will be more apt to receive with profit a lesson which seems to flow from the heart of the teacher rather than mere words from a book.

Guidelines: Memorize the memory verse and point out the deep feeling of humility we should have as we bow before our Creator. Before God we are like sheep to their shepherd. Describe the omnipresence of Jehovah God and how He watches over all His children and knows even their thoughts while they are afar off (1 Pet. 3:12; Psa. 139:1-2).

I. Daniel Worshipped God Faithfully

Emphasize the fact that Daniel, while he was very young, learned about God and the importance of faithful worship to Him. He did not wait until he was carried away captive. Explain how good character and right attitudes are molded at a very young age which will help us to choose what is right when we are older and the evil days of temptation come into our lives (Eccl. 12:1).

It may look like things are not going to turn out right for God's children sometimes. Yet, if we remember always to love God with all our hearts and to worship and serve Him faithfully all the days of our lives, all things will work together for our good (Rom. 8:28; Eccl. 7:8). The end is what really matters after all is said and done. In the end, the righteous will always be rewarded in a good way and the wicked will always be punished.

II. Mary and Joseph Worshipped Faithfully

The parents of Jesus were faithful in their worship to God. Point out that God does not judge a man by the kind of clothes he wears or the amount of money he has or gives, but by his faithful service unto Him (1 Sam. 16:7). A man may be poor in this world's goods but rich in his faith toward God (Jas. 2:5). The same man will always be pleasing and acceptable unto God. Explain that the turtledoves were an alternative gift when the worshippers could not afford the price of a lamb (Lev. 12:8).

III. Tips for the Teacher

Master this lesson before you attempt to teach it. Remember, if you do not know the way, you will be unprepared to teach and lead others. The reward of consecrated and painstaking preparation is worth much more than all the effort expended. Be sure you are a faithful worshipper of God yourself. If one is not trying to practice what he teaches, he is unworthy to lead others. Strive always to maintain respect from your students.

Answers in Lesson 8
Exercise 1. Fill In The Blanks:
1. Jerusalem, feast, passover (Luke 2:41)
2. serve, continually (Dan. 6:(16, 20)
3. God, angel, innocent (Dan. 6:22)
4. God, Judge (Bible Dictionary)
5. fault, faithful (Dan. 6:4)
6. governors, satraps, excellent spirit (Dan. 6:3)
7. feared, assembly, reverence (Ps. 89:7)
8. worship, only, serve (Matt. 4:10)
9. spirit, truth (John 4:24)
10. purposed, heart (Dan. 1:8)

Exercise 2. Match the Following: Dan. 1:1-8; 6:1-24
1. g (1:4)
2. e (1:3)
3. k (1:4)
4. b (1:4)
5. a (1:4)
6. j (6:16, 20)
7. i (1:3)
8. c (6:4)
9. f (6:10)
10. d (6:22)
11. h (6:22)

Exercise 3. For Class Discussion:

The king made a law forbidding Daniel to worship God. This forced Daniel to have to choose between God and the king. We must always prefer God's law over man's law when man's law conflicts with the law of God (Acts 5:27-29). Daniel did the king no hurt (Dan. 6:22). He was faithful in his service to the king until the king made a request that he could not conscientiously obey. Show the importance of having favor both with God and man (Acts 2:47; 24:16). A true child of God can associate to some extent with any rightful relationship in this world and still maintain his uncompromising devotion to God.

Notes

Lesson 9

A Virtuous Life

The Lesson Plan: "Yet he who reigns within himself, and rules passions, desires, and fears, is more a king; which every wise and virtuous man attains" (Milton's *Paradise Regained*). The aim of this lesson is to show that true moral excellence, as God sees it, is not just outward in the flesh, but inward as exemplified in a beautiful life. Show how a man who rules over his flesh is better than a hero who can capture a city (Prov. 16:32). The early indoctrination of our young people with the burning desire to do right above all else cannot be overly emphasized. This is a foundation principle of righteousness. Emphasize repeatedly that we must have the will and determination to do God's will all the time, no matter where we are or whatever may happen to us.

Explain how many will make fun of and ridicule you for having the courage to do right. Yet, deep inside, they really admire and respect anyone who has the will and determination to do what is right (1 Pet. 4:3-5; 3:14-16; 2:11-12).

Show how a virtuous life cannot be attained by mere good intentions. We must resolve and practice what is right over and again every day of the year. Explain how Christians pray to God and study His word for daily strength. It would be well to start each day with a prayer to God asking His help that we may do His will and for courage to let our inner spirit rule over our outward flesh.

Scripture Texts: Scripture selections have been chosen which show the moral excellence of both Daniel and Esther. The main texts are: Esther 2:5-20; 4:11-17; Daniel 1:1-8. Individual passages appear elsewhere throughout the text to help strengthen the theme of our study. Emphasize the point that both Daniel and Esther chose what they knew to be right even in the face of danger to their own lives. Explain how they both had the will and determination to do what is right before they were faced with the decisions they had to make. If we wait until danger comes before we determine to do right, it will then be too late. Both Daniel and Esther listened to and profited from their early training at home (Esth. 2:20; Dan. 1:4).

Guidelines: Memorize the memory verse and emphasize that we are and will become what we think about the most. If we think about cheap and ugly things long enough the same will be observed in our lives. ". . . for out of the abundance of the heart the mouth speaks" (Matt. 12:34b). In Philippians 4:8-9, Paul encouraged the Philippians to do what they had thought about, and what they had both learned, and received, and heard, and seen in him. Make the children see and feel the importance of deciding *now* to be the right kind of person with the will and determination to do the right things for the rest of their lives come what may. "Virtue" is defined by *World Book Dictionary*.

I. Daniel: A Virtuous Man

Give emphasis to the point that a virtuous life is better by far than a beautiful body or a keen mind. No matter how strong our body may be, it will return to dust. No matter how keen our mind may be, it will not function in this life after we depart. But virtue as a principle of righteousness will benefit us even after this life is over. It will ensure our everlasting happiness with God in the world to come. Tell how Solomon experienced almost everything this life can offer and concluded that all is vanity and striving after the wind. Give his final advice to all the living and especially to the very young (Eccl. 12:1, 13-14).

II. Esther: A Virtuous Woman

Often when a person grows up and leaves home he tends to forget his early training. This is true especially when riches, honor, and fame are set before one's eyes. However, if the desire to do right is strong enough, nothing can keep you from your determination to do what is right. Esther was a queen, but she thought more of doing right for her people than she did for her own safety.

III. Tips for the Teacher

The most valuable gift you can give your class is a good example. Kipling wrote, "Teach us to rule ourselves alway, controlled and cleanly night and day." The eyes of your students will be upon you – the teacher. Show the same will and determination in your faithfulness to the Lord that you are trying to provoke in the lives of your students.

IV. A Word of Encouragement.

A teacher's work is never done and many times it may seem like a thankless job. But we are promised that our work is not in vain in the Lord (1 Cor. 15:58). The teacher who really gets the point across is the one who does a little more preparation and presents the lesson a little more enthusiastically than is necessary and keeps on doing it! Fruit will be borne to the glory of God. It will be seen in the lives of the children you teach.

Answers in Lesson 9
Exercise 1. True and False:

1. True (Gal. 5:17)
2. False (Dan. 1:8)
3. False (Phil. 4:8)
4. True (Esth. 4:16)
5. False (Esth. 2:20)

Exercise 2. Complete the Puzzle:

The word under the star is *virtue*.

1. Vashti
2. Daniel
3. Mordecai
4. Esther
5. Ahasuerus
6. Heart

Exercise 3. For Class Discussion:

Try to show that we are and become what we think. (See Guidelines above.) The passages in Matthew 12:34b and Proverbs 3:5 teach that all our thoughts and actions originate in our heart. Explain that the Bible "heart" is the mind of man which is part of God's image in him.

Notes

Lesson 10
Fair Play

The Lesson Plan: "The best manner of avenging ourselves is by not resembling him who has injured us" (Jane Porter). The aim of this lesson is to impress upon the child's mind that it is right at all times to practice fair play and that it is never right to seek revenge. Stress the fact that the one who returns evil for evil always ends up getting hurt much worse. When life on earth is over, the righteous will be delivered from trouble and the avenging man will stand in trouble eternally (Prov. 11:8). Emphasize the absolute necessity of following in the steps of Christ (1 Pet. 2:21-24). Show how He practiced fair play even with His enemies. He left all vengeance to God who judges righteously. Stress the fact that God will bring every evil doer and every evil work into Judgment (Ecc. 12:14; Jude 14-15).

Scripture Tests: The scripture texts selected for this lesson illustrate both negatively and positively the subject of fair play. The main texts are: Genesis 50:15-21; Esther 3:1-6; 5; 7. Other scripture references relating to the subject will appear throughout the workbook. Fair play is always a timely and very important subject. To have a good lesson will require careful planning and preparation. Study to make your points clear to the students. Be enthusiastic!

Guidelines: Memorize the memory verse and impress upon the young minds that it is never right to hate one's neighbor. We should try rather to understand and to help him. Joseph was much happier himself and became a blessing to many people after he showed mercy toward his own brethren (Gen. 45:5; 50:20). He preserved life for himself and his entire family. "Fair play" and "vengeance" are both defined by the *World Book Dictionary*. Allow the students to express themselves and show how they can practice fair play towards one another in everyday life. Impress the fact that God knows all we say and do at all times.

I. Haman and Mordecai

The story of Haman and Mordecai illustrates clearly what happens to a person who fails to show mercy and fair play to his fellow man. Haman was very unhappy because he did not show mercy to Mordecai (Esth. 5:12-13). Note again the memory verse. Mordecai did not try to strike back at Haman, but made an appeal for his own life and simply ignored the man who was trying to harm him. After he was exposed, Haman feared what would happen to him (7:7). The fear of the wicked, in contrast to the peaceful mind of the righteous, is illustrated well in the Proverbs (10:6, 24).

II. Joseph and His Brethren

This story clearly shows that when we do wrong we will live in constant dread and fear of being found out (Gen. 42:21). Even though Joseph had many hardships during his life, all things worked together for his good because he loved the Lord and showed mercy and fair play towards his brethren. No one has ever gained anything by cheating or being unfair. All is well that ends well if it is right. It will never be well with us if we are always trying to get even with somebody who has done us wrong. We must pray to the Lord for strength to help us to be merciful and to practice fair play towards our fellow man at all times. Never return evil for evil. God will punish severely the one who does wrong.

III. Tips for the Teacher

Pray for wisdom to teach this lesson effectively. We must remember that we are teaching eternal souls and not just a lesson. Each child represents a challenge for you to communicate God's truth to their mind and to stimulate that mind to live and act accordingly. The better prepared you are and the more you make this lesson yours, the better you will be able to teach the child.

Answers in Lesson 10
Exercise 1. Match the Following:

1. d (Esth. 7:5)
2. a (Esth. 3:1; 7:6)
3. j (Esth. 7:9)
4. f (Esth. 2:7)
5. h (Esth. 5:14)
6. b (Esth. 7:9)
7. i (Gen. 50:20)
8. e (Esth. 7:6)
9. g (Matt. 7:12)
10. c (Rom. 12:19)

Exercise 2. Fill in the Blanks:

1. Mordecai, Haman, homage (Esth. 3:4)
2. favor, golden sceptre (Esth. 5:5)
3. life, people (Esth. 7:3)
4. adversary, enemy, Haman (Esth. 7:6)
5. Haman, Mordecai (Esth. 7:10)
6. repay, evil (Rom. 12:17)
7. Joseph, afraid, God (Gen. 50:19)
8. kind, happy (Prov. 14:21)
9. vengeance, Lord (Rom. 12:19)
10. words, blood, mouth (Prov. 12:6)

Exercise 3. True and False:

1. True (Esth. 5:14)
2. False (Gen. 50:15)
3. False (Rom. 12:19)
4. True (Gen. 50:20)
5. True (Prov. 14:21)

Exercise 4. For Class Discussion:

The saying, "Give a man enough rope and he will hang himself," can be easily explained with the Bible example of Haman and Mordecai. Haman set out to hang Mordecai and he ended up being hanged from his own gallows. When a person tries to get revenge for some unkind word or deed, he will always lose in the end. We soon become as bad as the person who did us wrong when we try to pay him back. Vengeance always belongs to God and He will give every man what he deserves. The scriptures in Proverbs and Ecclesiastes illustrate the

Notes

above saying in other words. We suffer both now and forever when we try to get revenge. We are happy now and forever when we try always to do what is right and leave all vengeance to the Lord. Illustrate your discussion from real life examples you know.

Lesson 11

Right Choices Assure Right Ends

The Lesson Plan: "He who chooses the beginning of a road chooses the place it leads to. It is the means that determines the end" (Harry Emerson Fosdick). The aim of this lesson is to impress indelibly upon the child's mind that "whatsoever a man soweth, that shall he also reap" (Gal. 6:7). There will be no personal exceptions. Encourage class participation throughout this lesson. First, involve yourself in the lesson and then seek to involve each individual student. Show personally how past choices have affected your life both in a good and bad way. Try to draw response from each child. Get the students talking among themselves about the lesson. Try to make them see that making choices in life is a very real and personal problem to them. Proceed then to help them find a solution for their personal problem.

Scripture Texts: The scripture texts selected for this lesson reveal the end result of both bad and good choices. The principle texts are: Genesis 13:5-13; Matthew 7:13-14; Hebrews 11:24-26. Other references will appear throughout the text to illustrate and emphasize the end of the choices we make.

Guidelines: Memorize the memory verse and emphasize the point that the end is better only when the beginning choice is right and good. No matter how good the beginning may seem, if the choice made at that time is not right, the end will be bad. On the other hand, if the beginning choice is right and good, no matter how bad it may seem at the time, the end will always be better. Illustrate this principle of righteousness from your own experience and draw on other illustrations from your students. Point out that the examples of choices made in this lesson are God's warning signs for us either to imitate or to avoid. The example of Adam and Eve eating the forbidden fruit is a good example to illustrate the saying, "all that glitters is not gold." The terrible consequences following the sin of Adam and Eve prove this to be so. We, too, will have to bear the consequences of our own sins.

I. Lot Failed to Look to the End of His Choice

The story of Lot illustrates the mistake of making a choice in view of only those present things that are before you and not looking to where those present things might lead. It points out the danger of just living for today and failing to watch out and prepare for tomorrow. Lot did not go immediately to Sodom but merely pitched his tent in that direction. Very soon he was all the way in Sodom. "Man cannot take fire in his bosom and his clothes not be burned" (Prov. 6:27-28). Likewise, he cannot go in the direction of sin without getting hurt. The Bible says Lot was vexed by the filthy conversation of the wicked (2 Pet. 2:7). God teaches us to avoid the very appearance of evil and to abhor that which is evil and cleave to that which is good (1 Thess. 5:22; Rom. 12:9). We must hate evil before we can love that which is good.

II. Moses Looked to the End of the Choices He Made

Notes

The wisdom of the world would say that Moses made a mistake when he turned down princehood, worldly pleasures, and the treasures of Egypt. However, we know Moses was truly wise when he looked to the end of his choice and had more respect for God's reward than what the world could offer. Moses could "see past his nose." He knew the wisdom of looking to the end of choices that were before him. The earthly honors, pleasures, and treasures of Egypt are now long gone but the reward Moses respected is still yet to come. Paul says the "sufferings of this present time are not worthy to be compared with the glory which shall be revealed hereafter" (Rom. 8:18).

III. The Two Ways

Each of us will travel one of the two ways the Lord described. Surely, according to the standards of the world, the broad way would be much more appealing in the beginning. But what about the other end? How many, when they reach the end of the broad way, do you suppose would give ten thousand worlds like this if they had chosen the narrow road when they made their beginning choice? The narrow road might appear hard to travel right now, but look at the other end. It leads to life everlasting where no one will be sorry.

IV. Tips for the Teacher

This lesson is very important but can be no more effective than the teacher who teaches it. By all means study well this lesson and know before class just how you plan to present the material in the most effective way to the children you have been assigned to teach. Make this lesson live in the hearts of your students. An impression you make while teaching this lesson may make the difference in the salvation of many souls! Pray without ceasing.

Answers to Lesson 11
Exercise 1. Fill in the Blanks:
1. pitched, tent, Sodom, Sodom, wicked, sinners, Lord (Gen. 13:12-13)
2. prince, pleasures, treasures, respect, reward (Heb. 11:24-26)
3. Abram, Lot, strife, herdsmen, brethren (Gen. 13:8)
4. tree, food, pleasant, eyes, tree, desired, wise (Gen. 3:6)
5. lacks, shortsighted, blindness, forgotten, sins (2 Pet. 1:9)

Exercise 2. True and False:
1. False (Eccl. 7:8)
2. True (Gal. 6:7)
3. False (Gen. 3:3)
4. False (Matt. 7:13-14)
5. True (Heb. 11:24-26)

Exercise 3. For Class Discussion:
Both Joshua and Elijah had the end in view when they pleaded with the children of Israel. Both men of God knew that God's children could not sow to the flesh without reaping corruption. In Joshua 24:20, Joshua describes what God would do to the children of Israel even after having blessed them. Elijah proved that the consequences of following Baal was certain destruction (1 Kings 18:40). The faithful never have any regrets.

Lesson 12

Forgiveness

The Lesson Plan: "To err is human; to forgive, divine" (Alexander Pope). The aim of this lesson is to raise the child from the human tendency to strike back to the higher and divine tendency to forgive. This principle of righteousness is a most important step in molding a young mind to be like Christ (1 Pet. 2:21). Impress upon the child's mind how spiteful acts, the holding of grudges, and hateful attitudes of getting even must be eliminated completely from the life of every Christian. An unforgiving spirit will result both in unhappiness in this life and eternal destruction in the life to come. Show how the attitude of forgiveness will help bring happiness to our lives and will help avoid unpleasantness with others (Matt. 5:7; Prov. 15:1). It also will move our enemies to shame (Prov. 25:21; Rom. 12:20).

Scripture Texts: The scripture texts selected for this lesson illustrate how good always results from the forgiving spirit. They include: Genesis 37; 45:1-15; 50:19-21; Luke 7:36-50; 23:34-45. Other scripture references will appear in the text. Be completely familiar with all scriptures in the workbook and be able to relate them to the subject. Study your lesson well and present it enthusiastically.

Guidelines: Memorize the memory verse and emphasize how God forgave man who was unworthy of His forgiveness. If God forgives us of our many sins, surely we can forgive one another. "Forgiveness" is defined by the *World Book Dictionary*. Ask for examples of forgiveness in the lives of your students. Let them tell how they have forgiven others and have helped to bring out good rather than hateful things in the lives of others.

I. Joseph Forgave His Brethren

Emphasize how our sins will always find us out (Num. 32:23). Show how the sins of envy and hatred always result in unhappiness and suffering both for yourself and for other people as well. The eleven brothers sinned against Joseph and their father. They had to carry the guilt of their sins in their hearts for many years before they finally found them out. In contrast, show how faithfulness to God always pays off. Describe the beauty of forgiveness. Put your heart into this beautiful lesson!

II. Jesus Forgave Many

Christ practiced what He preached to His disciples. When godly sorrow worked repentance in an individual's life, Jesus was ready to forgive them. Christ gave Peter the opportunity to express his love for Him (John 21:15-17). Jesus appointed work for Peter to do to prove his love. Christ's forgiveness of the sinful woman and the thief illustrates how He is able and will forgive even the vilest sinner who is truly sorry and repents (Heb. 7:25). Show how God wants all men to be saved and is ready to forgive them if they will repent and come to the knowledge of the truth (2 Pet. 3:9; 1 Tim. 2:4). Christ showed His willingness to

Notes

forgive even those who crucified Him. To have the spirit of Christ, we must be willing to forgive both those who ask forgiveness and those who do not ask. Jesus and Stephen did.

III. Lesson to Learn:

Emphasize here that failure to forgive is a form of selfishness on our part. This would be a good place to emphasize the golden rule (Matt. 7:12). Also point out that true happiness comes by giving rather than from receiving (Acts 20:35). This thought can be effectively woven throughout the lesson. Stress the fact that an unmerciful and unforgiving person cannot be saved.

IV. Tips for the Teacher:

A big responsibility in the teaching process is to stimulate the self-activities of the student. The teacher can be most helpful in this by asking pertinent questions and allowing the student freely to express himself. The child will be encouraged to think for himself and will become a searcher for truth with the proper guidance. Help the child to make practical applications of the lesson in his everyday life.

Answers in Lesson 12
Exercise 1. Fill in the Blanks

1. Reuben, Judah, brother, flesh (Gen. 37:22, 27)
2. Dan, Naphtali, Gad, Asher (Gen. 37:2; 35:25-26)
3. son, old age, Rachel (Gen. 37:3; 35:24)
4. envied, observed (Gen. 37:11)
5. Stephen, Lord, sin (Acts 7:60)
6. Midianites, Potiphar, officer, Pharoah's (Gen. 37:36)
7. grieved, angry, God (Gen. 45:5)
8. Christ, Stephen (Luke 23:34, Acts 7:54-60)
9. today, paradise (Luke 23:43)
10. sins, forgiven, loved (Luke 7:47)

Exercise 2. True and False

1. True (Luke 7:39-47)
2. False (Gen. 37:9-10)
3. False (James 2:13)
4. True (Gen. 45:5, 7; 50:20)
5. True (Rom. 8:28)
6. False (Gen. 37:20-22; 26-27)

Exercise 3. For Class Discussion

1. Joseph typified Christ in several ways. Some of their likenesses were as follows: They both were

   a. Hated—Gen. 37:4, 5; John 7:7
   b. Conspired against—Gen. 37:18; Matt. 26:4
   c. Mocked—Gen. 37:19, 23; Matt. 27:29
   d. Sold—Gen. 37:27; Mark 14:10
   e. Reported dead—Gen. 37:31; Mark 15:44
   f. Raised and exalted—Gen. 41; Phil. 2:9
   g. Forgiving—Gen. 45:5, 7; 50:20; Luke 23:34, 43

2. When people say hurtful things to us because we are Christians we must learn to ignore it as Jesus did (cf. Luke 6:22-23; 1 Pet. 2:11-12; 3:14-16; 4:4). The reward later will make it all worth while (Rom. 8:18).

Lesson 13
Meekness: The Crowning Principle

The Lesson Plan: "Even the man Moses, the meekest of men, was wrathful sometimes" (George Eliot). "Meekness is like one of those flagrant trees which bathes with its perfume the axe that smites into its wood. The meek man gives back love for hate, kindness for unkindness, sweetness for bitterness" (J. R. Miller). The aim of this lesson is to convince all present that meekness is indeed the crowning principle of righteousness. Emphasize over and over again that meekness is not weakness but true strength under control. Encourage the class to participate with you, the teacher, in learning about this most important subject. Ask the class for examples they know that illustrate the principle in their own lives. If you can get a good feedback from your students you can teach them so they will not soon forget. Make the class see that it takes real manhood and womanhood to keep still and hold your tongue when somebody insults you or hurts your feelings. Remember that Christ always was able to do this and left for us this most important example.

Scripture Texts: The scripture texts selected for this lesson illustrate in the lives of Moses, Christ, and Stephen the principle of meekness. In each case, note with the class the absence of any weakness and the presence of real strength. The principle texts are: Numbers 12; Matthew 11:28-30; Acts 7:51-60. Other references will appear throughout the lesson to support the main points. Read them all and be familiar with every passage.

Guidelines: Memorize the memory verse and point out that only the truly meek will seek after the Lord and will therefore inherit the earth (Matt. 5:5). The definition of "meekness" is taken from the *World Book Dictionary*. Emphasize the point that the truly meek person overlooks any personal injury done him. He never holds a grudge. Therefore, he is nearly always happy and pleasant. Whereas, a person who is easily offended and holds grudges against others is nearly always unhappy and unpleasant to be around.

I. The Meekness of Moses

Moses is the greatest example of meekness in the entire Old Testament. There is absolutely no indication that he ever became angry because of personal insult or injury. Yet, he was always quick to defend any principle of righteousness that was violated. He was always quick to defend a fellow creature who was wounded or under the threat of being destroyed. Make a practical application from the life of Moses to the class. Let the class help you do this. Get feedback.

II. The Meekness of Christ

Teach from the meekness of Christ the difference in personal injury and the violation of a principle. Why take personal injury lightly and become angry when principles are violated? The answer is obvious. What happens to us personally will not matter after a while. Yet, when princi-

Notes

ples of righteousness are violated they have eternal consequences. For example, it is just as wrong today to show disrespect for God and His word as it was in the days of Moses or Christ. Therefore, being angry at the right time is to be angry when attitudes and actions that affect our eternal salvation are wrong. This is why it is not personal when we become angry as Jesus did with the scribes and Pharisees. If His anger were personal, He could not be angry one minute and pray for them the next. This principle is true in all three examples in our lesson. Make this point clear to the students.

III. The Meekness of Stephen

Again, Stephen could see that the attitude of those listening to him would cause them to be lost on the day of Judgment, if they did not repent. Yet, he was not personally angry with them because we find him praying for them as they stoned him to death. If we can pray for those who persecute us, we will not be personally angry or hold a grudge against them.

IV. Tips for the Teacher

Much time and prayer has gone into the preparation and writing of this lesson. Please pray yourself and spend enough time on this lesson that it will flow easily from your soul as you face those young minds at class time. This very lesson may be the key that unlocks a future of happiness and eventual salvation for those who learn well its meaning. Be enthusiastic in your teaching.

Answers in Lesson 13
Exercise 1. Fill in the Blanks:

1. Moses, humble, face (Num. 12:3)
2. Moses, heal, pray (Num. 12:13)
3. Father's, house, merchandise (John 2:16)
4. Anger, grieved, hardness, hand (Mark 3:5)
5. Prophets, fathers, Just One, betrayers, murderers (Acts 7:52)
6. Stephen, loud, Lord, sin, charge (Acts 7:60)
7. Yoke, learn, gentle, lowly, souls (Matt. 11:29)
8. Reviled, suffered, committed, Him, judges (1 Pet. 2:23)

Exercise 2. For Class Discussion:

1. Read Matthew 10:28. What man may do to us personally will not affect our eternal salvation. The wrong attitude and action on our part will affect our salvation. Therefore, righteous anger directed against wrong attitudes and actions is proper and expected with a view toward saving the one who is in the wrong.

2. Righteous anger is soon over. Personal anger lingers. One who reacts to personal injuries is not likely to pray for the one who offended him as did Moses, Christ, and Stephen.

Lesson 1
Paul's Early Life

Begin by introducing the book as a whole to the class explaining the overall purpose which is stated by the title: "Paul and His Companions." You may quickly thumb through the book to give them a bird's-eye view of subjects to be studied this quarter.

When You Complete This Lesson You Should Know

This particular section of the lesson will always set forth the aims of the lesson. Prepare your lesson so as to develop these points, and you will usually succeed in teaching the lesson. You will find it much easier to emphasize a few major points than to discuss a lesson at random with a multitude of points. When you finish the lesson you should review briefly, perhaps by questions you have written, to see if the class has learned the major points.

Paul's Birthplace and Education

Either you, or one of the students, should read the Scripture Text aloud to the class. You will probably find it easy to tie the Scripture Text in with a discussion of this section in the study books. It will be of interest to the students for you to locate on the map Paul's birthplace, Tarsus, and show its relation geographically to Jerusalem and Rome. Do some research on Tarsus to explain how that it was "no mean city." Particularly establish the point that every person born in that city was automatically a Roman citizen. Explain the privileges of being a Roman citizen. Not all Jews were Romans, but Paul was one because of his place of birth. You may wish to develop what a great advantage his Roman citizenship proved to be later, as he was imprisoned at Philippi and then when he used the right of appeal to Caesar.

Develop Paul's early life as a Jew being taught by Gamaliel. Help the students gain an understanding of some of the reasons why Paul could be so fervent in thinking he was serving God by persecuting Christians. Emphasize his good conscience in persecuting Christians and apply that to present day situations, showing that one can be honestly mistaken in religious error. This, of course, leads you to the conclusion stressing the need to study the Bible diligently to make certain we believe the truth. Also, point out that Paul was a sinner needing forgiveness even though his conscience was clear, and show how this is unlike some modern teaching.

Paul's Conversion to Christ

Explain that, with a clear conscience and zeal for God, Paul was on the way to Damascus. It was this honest attitude that enabled him to believe when he saw, for the first time, that Christ was, in fact, the Son of God. Take the diagram of what Paul did to become a Christian, pausing between each step to compare with the various false doctrines taught today for salvation. Show that many preachers might claim we can be saved by doing any one of the things on the left, but that, even with all of them put together, Paul still needed to be baptized. This is a

Paul and His Companions

Notes

good time to develop the purpose for baptism which can be seen in the memory verse. Have several students quote the verse in class and encourage all of them to work every week to memorize the selected verse before class. Go over the True-False exercise and Crossword Puzzle and discuss each question to see if the students understand the correct answers.

Lesson 2

Paul, A Worker for Christ

Begin the class by briefly reviewing "Paul's Early Life."

When You Complete This Lesson You Should Know

This states the aim of the lesson, therefore, prepare your class so as to develop these significant points. This lesson is a broad study on the life of Paul as a Christian. It is an easy lesson in which to become bogged down on a single thought, but this must be avoided by keeping in mind that we are simply trying to give the student a general, overall view of the life of Paul as a worker for Christ.

You may want to discuss the Scripture Text verse by verse, but probably you will not have time to read all the verses and will need to be acquainted well enough with the text to tell the story in your own words. The reason this scripture text was selected is because it tells Paul's life from his early years, how he was converted, and then that the only reason he was made a prisoner is because he preached and worked for Christ. Tie in the memory verse with this Scripture Text. Emphasize the thought of the memory verse, asking several students to quote it in class. Discuss its meaning, making sure they know more than just the words of the verse. This verse best describes the goal of our lesson—the idea that Paul gave himself for Christ (crucified with him) and was a worker for Christ.

A Chosen Vessel

You may need to read the story in the book to the class, but if the students have properly prepared you shouldn't. In fact, the questions were arranged so that the student would have to read the lesson story at least twice to find the answers. After discussing this particular section you can check their work on the exercise on drawing the wavy line, putting a circle around, etc. That will determine how well they have prepared the lesson and whether or not they have gotten the main points from the lesson story. Avoid getting off on one particular point. Remember, the chief design of the lesson is to emphasize Paul's whole life as a worker, who crucified himself that Christ might live in him.

After you have completed the lesson story see if the students can quote all the books of the New Testament. Assign them the task of learning them if they do not already know all. Test their knowledge of the books Paul wrote. You may develop the point that these books actually inform us in more detail about the life of Paul, though they were written to churches and individuals. Our memory verse was written by Paul and it tells us his attitude toward the work of Christ, and also the scripture we used from 2 Timothy which shows his attitude toward death. The book of Acts tells us the life of Paul from a historical point of view, but the books Paul wrote tell us various events about his life from his own point of view. Paul's books were written earlier than any other New Testament book.

Notes

Preaching Journeys

This lesson will probably require the most skill on your part as the teacher in getting across what is desired. Any lesson which covers a broad view of Paul's life must make some mention of his journeys. Certainly several weeks are necessary to cover these trips in detail, so you must work at being able, in one lesson, to give your students an overall view of his trips in detail without making them feel "burdened down" with too many facts and cities to be remembered. Later we shall talk in more detail about these journeys as we discuss Paul's companions. However, in this lesson we simply want to acquaint the student generally, briefly, and in as simple a manner as we can with the journeys that Paul took in preaching the gospel. Let them see something of the geography where he travelled. You may, for example, explain that Paul's first journey covered about 1300-1400 miles and took about four and a half years. The second journey covered better than 2000 miles and took about three years while the third journey also covered more than 2000 miles and took about four and a half years. Then you may apply this by illustrating from where you live how far a round trip like that would take. Emphasize the difference in mode of travel from our modern means. The ships, being sailboats, depended on the current or wind to move them, and travel over land was often by foot, making journeys both slow and difficult. Give them the illustration to emphasize how devoted Paul must have been to take these journeys. Paul stayed various lengths of time at the places he visited.

This last exercise is simply to get the students to look at the map and be introduced to his journeys. (You should have a large map in the class room.) It may be difficult if the student does not look carefully at the lines to distinguish where Paul went on each separate journey. Be careful to note which cities Paul visited more than once. Conclude your lesson by emphasizing the aim of the lesson to see if they have learned these major points.

Lesson 3

Barnabas, A Good Man

Begin the class by briefly reviewing the lesson on "Paul, A Worker For Christ."

When You Complete This Lesson You Should Know

The aim of this lesson is to give the student an understanding of the close relationship Barnabas had with Paul, and how he befriended him in the beginning and worked hand in hand with him for several years. Also, we want to make the lesson have a practical application for our lives by emphasizing the character of Barnabas as a good man. The students should know what is involved in being a good man, in the Bible sense, and then ask themselves if they are striving to be "good" in the sense that the Lord is directing all their steps.

A Co-Worker With Paul

You may begin by discussing the lesson story as it follows a chronological order of Barnabas in his relationship with Paul. You may wish to begin by discussing the last point made in the lesson concerning his name. The ASV translates the meaning as "Son of Exhortation" while the NASB translates his name as "Son of Encouragement." It is an interesting point to observe how Barnabas encouraged and exhorted others to be faithful. In his first relationship with Paul, Barnabas encouraged him by befriending him when the other disciples at Jerusalem were afraid of Paul. And again, it was Barnabas who was the encouraging man who went to Tarsus to bring Saul to Antioch to work with him.

If you feel you have time, you may wish to select some key verses from Acts 13 and 14 to give the students a general view of the places Paul visited and the events that occurred on the first preaching journey. It would be good to use a map to illustrate where they travelled, as well as the relationship of Antioch to both Tarsus and Jerusalem.

Visual aids are always effective, especially with the junior age group. If you can devise other aids to use, such as flannel graph or blackboard material, you will find that it will add much to making a lasting impression in the memory of your students.

The exercises at the end of this first section will serve as a barometer to determine how well they have grasped the relationship of Barnabas to Paul. The second exercise, "Draw A Line To The Circle," will particularly emphasize how many things the Bible tells us that Paul and Barnabas did together and should make the student realize that, with this much work common to both men, they must have greatly influenced the lives of each other.

A Good Man

This section of the lesson will be the most important in giving the students a practical lesson for their own lives. You may expand the thought of what is involved in being a good man. The world appreciates

Notes

good men, but usually this term is applied only to those who are kind and thoughtful of others. Make the application that God wants us to be good in this sense, but that He expects more of us. You may contrast the rich young ruler and his failure to obey (Matt. 19:16-22) with Cornelius who did obey (Acts 10:1-2; 11:14; 10:48). Show that both men were good morally and good neighbors, but that only one of them, Cornelius, was good in the sense that he pleased God and would have the promise of eternal life. Make a distinct point of the fact that not all good people—as the world thinks of the term—are Christians.

Another practical application is the lesson of generosity. Barnabas sold his land to give to the needy, and we must also be of the same mind when there is need. The true meaning of generosity is not what is given but what is left. The poor widow cast in only two mites but gave more than others who cast much into the treasury (Mark 12:41-44). Show the meaning of sacrifice and ask ourselves the question, "How much can I afford to keep?" rather than "How much do I have to give?" (2 Cor. 9:6-7). True goodness must be willing to sacrifice for God. Even this age group should begin to think about giving to God and teach them to purpose to give a portion of their weekly allowance or money which they may earn for doing errands.

Conclude your lesson by summing up the chief points you have discussed and through reading again Acts 11:24—"a great many people were added to the Lord." Be sure to test the students on whether or not they have learned this memory verse and check their answers for the last section of questions.

Lesson 4

John Mark, the Man Who Turned Back

Begin by briefly reviewing the lesson, "Barnabas, A Good Man."

When You Complete This Lesson You Should Know

Perhaps the title of this lesson is not a fair description of the impression we want to leave about John Mark. It is significant that he turned back and that Paul and Barnabas separated over him for this reason. However, we need to develop from that incident the character of a man who may have faltered, but was certainly not a failure. Perhaps you can develop the point that all human beings have their weaknesses and none of us has achieved sinless perfection. We need the encouragement of an example like John Mark who overcame his weaknesses to become a successful and faithful follower of Christ. Although Paul once refused to take him on his second journey, he later wrote to Timothy desiring that he bring Mark with him because Mark had proven to be useful to him in the ministry.

The memory verse has been selected as one taken from the book written by Mark. Of course, it is an important thought to emphasize and memorize. You may wish to drill the class at the beginning of the lesson to see how well they have learned this verse.

A Cousin to Barnabas

Develop the idea of the home life Mark must have had and the blessing of being raised by a godly mother. You may go into a brief account of why Peter was in prison and how the Lord provided his escape. Tell also how Rhoda ran back into the house for joy, leaving Peter outside the locked gate. But in the telling of this story continue to tie this in with the fact that it happened at the house of Mark's mother. Explain, too, that one may be described in a spiritual sense as a "son" like Peter described Mark (cf. 1 Cor. 4:14-15). Mark's relation to Barnabas is confusing if reading the KJV ("sister's son" sounds as though he is a nephew). However, the Greek word used, *anepsios*, denotes a cousin rather than a nephew and is so translated in revised versions of the N.T. In this sense it is used in the Septuagint (Greek O.T.) in Numbers 36:11 *(Expository Dictionary of N.T. Words by W. E. Vine)*.

Paul and Barnabas Separate Over Mark

As you tell of the separation of these two great men over Mark emphasize the point that their disagreement was over a matter of judgment and that they did not cause division in the Lord's church, for such was condemned (1 Cor. 1:10-13). Teach a lesson that, in matters of judgment, we may sometimes disagree but in matters of faith, we must always be united through submitting our minds to the will of Christ.

Avoid being dogmatic as to the reason Mark turned back. The Scriptures do not indicate his motive. True, Paul thought it was not justified, at least not enough to take him again. However, Barnabas thought he was worthy to be taken again. We do not know the Lord's view of the matter and we must not venture an opinion that would say either Paul

Notes

or Barnabas was correct. Leave the point simply that it was over this cause that they separated, and Barnabas took Mark with him to Cyprus.

Mark, A Useful Minister

This is the point in the lesson which must be developed for application to your students. Showing that Mark evidently proved himself and continued to stand for the truth should be an encouragement for us to persevere. We shouldn't be "quitters" because we make a few mistakes. Nor should we get our feelings hurt and bear grudges because someone has become disappointed with us. Paul later referred to Mark as a "comfort" to him and as a "fellow laborer," so we know Mark was surely a "useful minister" to Paul.

You may impress the fact that the book of Mark was written by this man. It may be good to have them say all the books of the New Testament if you have time.

Finish the class by checking their work on the crossword puzzle.

Lesson 5

Silas, Chosen for Paul's Second Journey

Begin by briefly reviewing the lesson, "John Mark, The Man Who Turned Back."

When You Complete This Lesson You Should Know

Silas is an important character to study as he was Paul's companion on his second missionary journey; however, the Bible does not give us a lot of detail about him. This lesson is designed, therefore, to acquaint the student with Silas, who he was as well as his connection with Paul. The exercises are designed to give the teacher an easy method of developing the aims of the lesson that are stated. Therefore, we suggest that, as you teach this lesson, you follow rather closely the pattern and material in the lesson book.

The Scripture Text and Memory Verse are both connected with the last point of the lesson, the conversion of the Philippian Jailer, so wait until you come to this point in your class to discuss the text or to have the students quote the verse.

A Chief Man Among the Brethren

As a teacher you must thoroughly acquaint yourself with the background of Acts 15:22-41; actually you would be best prepared by reading a good commentary on the whole chapter of Acts 15. However, to reach the goals of this lesson you must not spend a lot of time giving a detailed account of this to the class, because you are likely to be more drawn into a discussion about the instructions to the Gentiles, which were contained in the letter from the elders and apostles, than about Silas himself. Briefly tell the chief points of this meeting in Jerusalem and show the importance of Silas by the fact that he was selected to travel with Paul and Barnabas. Such a grave matter required a capable and respected man. The exercise will cause the student to read this account at least once and draw his attention to the verses in which Silas is mentioned.

Paul's Second Preaching Journey

You cannot expect to cover in great detail every event of this journey; however, the purpose in mind is to give the student an overall view of what occurred. If he is acquainted in this quarter with the life of Paul as a whole, then in later studies he will be better prepared to study in greater detail such events as the second journey. Keeping in mind that we want a survey of this second journey, you should have a good map before the class and be able to relate, in your own words the places Paul and Silas visited and the most important events which took place. The exercise, "Who, Where, and What" should help you in selecting the chief points to develop. As you prepare for the class, determine how much time you intend to devote to each section of this study and then you will be able to know how brief (or detailed) you will be. Sometimes teachers get bogged down in lessons of this sort and spend several weeks trying to cover the material. Avoid doing this. You will

Notes

have missed the purpose in mind if it takes you more than one lesson to cover this second journey. We realize they will not have much detail, but that is not our purpose now.

An interesting point that is not developed in the lesson is the mention of "Silvanus" in 2 Corinthians 1:19 and in the introduction of both 1 and 2 Thessalonians. "Silvanus" is the same as "Silas."

Conversion of the Philippian Jailer

This example of conversion is important to understand and, since Silas was involved, we have chosen to include its detailed account in this lesson. This is the part of the lesson with application for the student. Your students are approaching the age of responsibility, and they should be well informed on what God expects of them in becoming a Christian. The Scripture Text should now be read, or perhaps you will have time left only to tell it in your own words or have one of the students to tell the story. The exercise should help you develop the points involved in becoming a Christian and furnishes you other verses to use. The Memory Verse is longer than usual but since the advocates of the doctrine of "faith only" always stop after verse 31, it is good for the student to memorize at an early age the rest of the passage, particularly that the same hour of the night the Jailer was baptized. You may stress how this suggests urgency in baptism and therefore does not conform to the idea in the doctrine of salvation by faith only.

Lesson 6

Timothy, the Young Evangelist

Begin the class by briefly reviewing "Silas, Chosen For Paul's Second Journey."

When You Complete This Lesson You Should Know

There are so many wonderful and valuable lessons to be learned from the study of Timothy that it will be difficult for the teacher to limit himself to two or three major points. However, we have tried to give a broad base in these three aims of the lesson and memory verse.

About Timothy's home and how he became acquainted with Paul. In developing this point the teacher may also teach the lesson of the value of God-fearing parents and the responsibilities of both parents and children in serving God. A good lesson for girls is to be drawn from the work done by Eunice and Lois. Surely the church would be blessed with more Timothy's, if only there were more devoted mothers like Eunice and Lois!

Of the unfeigned faith in Timothy. The teacher may expand this lesson to encourage young men to have the goal in life to preach the gospel. They need to be filled with the encouragement necessary to make the choice for this work. Those with "unfeigned faith" evaluate the things most necessary and important in life and can be molded into diligent servants of the Lord.

Paul's feelings toward Timothy. The whole basis for this study is Timothy's relationship to Paul, and we could not have learned about Timothy except that we know something of Paul's affection for him and their companionship. However, in this section you may emphasize the lesson of being "likeminded" as Timothy to truly put the Lord's work first.

Memory Verse: You may draw a fourth major lesson from this verse in teaching the completeness of the word of God and of our need to follow the inspired Scriptures without addition or subtraction. This is a longer memory verse than usual, but the children of Junior age are at their most rapid learning period and should be able to commit this to memory rather easily.

Timothy Accompanies Paul and Silas

It would be good to use a map again to illustrate where Lystra is located, pointing out, too, that Paul and Barnabas were together when they went there on the first missionary journey. You may also remind them that this city is where Paul was stoned and left for dead (Acts 14:8-20). No doubt Timothy saw this as a young man and it surely made a deep impression on him. Make the point that the Scriptures do not actually say that Paul converted Timothy but that Paul does refer to him as a "son in the gospel" which would indicate such.

If you have time in the class you may have the students turn to the six books in which Paul associates Timothy in his writing and have them read aloud the salutations.

Notes

Timothy's Unfeigned Faith

If you do have time for extra reading in the class you may also have them read some of the admonitions from 1 and 2 Timothy, particularly the "underlying messages" (e.g. 1 Tim. 4:12-16; 6:12; 2 Tim. 1:13; 2:22-26; 4:2-5).

Of course, you would want to read the scripture text of 2 Timothy 1:1-6 and discuss its meaning, particularly emphasizing the kind of faith Timothy had which first was in his mother and grandmother. Also, teach about the affection Paul showed for Timothy.

No Man Likeminded

This text is a good one to make application for our own lives in teaching the need for whole hearted service to the Lord. Timothy's attitude would certainly be unique in our age as well as in the days of Paul. While men are busy here and there with "their own" interests, the most important thing is the work of Christ. We should never be too busy to study, to worship, to care for the needy, or to teach the lost. Attempt to draw your students into discussing ways in which men seek 'their own' interests today rather than the things of the Lord and ask them for suggestions of how to apply this to our own lives.

Lesson 7

Titus, A Man of Faith and Order

Begin by briefly reviewing "Timothy, the Young Evangelist."

When You Complete This Lesson You Should Know

These aims of the lesson should be rather easily developed from the scripture texts and lesson story. Actually, the Bible does not give us a biography of Titus, and information concerning him is somewhat patchwork. However, the main impression we want to leave with the students is his companionship to Paul and the importance he maintained in being a "fellowhelper."

The memory verse can be brought into the lesson either at the first or last of the class period, according to your own discretion. The thought of it does not directly relate to the life of Titus, but since it is found in the book of Titus and a good lesson within itself, the students should commit these verses to memory. You may find it a good text from which to draw a practical lesson for the class on how God expects us to live righteous lives, denying the things of the world.

Titus, a Gentile Convert of Paul

You may wish to have this section of the lesson story either read aloud in class or summarized. The purpose in this section is to establish who Titus was and his early relationship with Paul. Through a process of deduction we know that Acts 15 and Galatians 2 must be parallel accounts of the same incident. Therefore, Titus was with Paul on the trip to Jerusalem. Depending on the maturity of your class, you may want to get into a discussion of why Paul circumcised Timothy but refused to circumcise Titus (Acts 16:1-3). The mother of Timothy was a Jewess and, because of the circumstances in which they were placed, Paul had Timothy circumcised. We can be certain that Timothy was not circumcised as a condition for salvation, but rather in order to keep him from being considered unclean. Paul refused to circumcise Titus, who was a Gentile, as its object would have been to bring him under the yoke of the law. One was more for social reasons and to be above losing influence regarding a matter of indifference, while the other would have been a matter of spiritual concern and whether or not circumcision was a necessity.

Paul's "Partner and Fellowhelper" to Corinth

Again, depending on the maturity of your class, you may wish to go into a brief detail of some of the problems that existed in Corinth (1 Cor. 5) and then show the ugly situation into which Titus was sent. Of course, this gives us insight into the reason for Paul's concern and then the deep joy he had at the good report of Titus. It also helps to understand more about the ability Titus must have had to handle such a matter. If your class is not mature enough for this depth of insight, it would be best to stay close to the lesson text as written, leaving most of your period for a discussion of the last section on the book of Titus itself.

Notes

The Book of Titus

There are so many good lessons to be drawn from the book of Titus itself that you could so arrange your class as to talk briefly about the first two sections and then spend most of the time emphasizing the book. Show on your map where the island of Crete is located.

The matching exercise is to cause the students to see some of the obvious similarities between 1 Timothy and Titus, while the last exercise gives emphasis to the qualifications of elders. You may wish to talk about elders, the extent of their oversight, and why it is so important that they meet these qualifications. This will be a good lesson to encourage young men to set the attaining of these qualifications as their goal. We tried to encourage young men to become preachers in our lesson on Timothy, and, in this lesson, it would fold in nicely to point out that all cannot be preachers, but that a higher work than that is to develop oneself to serve as a faithful bishop. We need to encourage young men in this, and the Junior level is at the most impressionable age to set such goals before them.

Lesson 8

Luke, The Beloved Physician

Begin the class by briefly reviewing "Titus, A Man of Faith and Order."

When You Complete This Lesson You Should Know

The New Testament does not give a biography of the life of Luke and, though he is the author of Acts, he does not even mention himself by name or tell of his personal involvement in the life of Paul. However, it is clear that he travelled with Paul. Therefore, we want to draw from the few passages available to point out Luke's companionship to Paul. Of special importance, however, is the fact that Luke is the author of both the book of Luke and the book of Acts, so one primary aim of this lesson is to give the class something that will cause them to remember this as well as what the two books are about.

The third aim, as stated, is about the conversion of Lydia. Both the scripture text and memory verse pertain to this incident and may be reserved for reading or quoting until you have reached that point in the lesson.

Luke, The Beloved Physician

You may have three of your students read these references where Luke is mentioned and show how that we know the occupation of Luke from Colossians 4:14. As you discuss his birthplace and whether or not Luke was a Gentile, remember that we cannot be dogmatic about this. History, or tradition, has left us with this information and it seems reliable enough to know, but it is not of such chief importance to spend a great deal of time on it or to be arbitrary.

It should be interesting to the class to be shown from the map the location of Troas and Philippi. Read the verses in Acts which indicate Luke was with Paul as indicated by the change from "they," "them" to "we," "us" and vice versa.

Writer of Luke and Acts

You may find the class curious to know how a man who was not an apostle could write the books of Luke and Acts. It seems that many have been left with the impression that only the apostles were inspired to write books of the New Testament. However, you can show that Luke, like Timothy, Titus, and others upon whom the apostles had laid hands, were given the miraculous gifts of the Holy Spirit (Acts 8:14-17; 1 Cor. 12:8-11; 13:9-13). Such men might well fit into the class of New Testament prophets to whom the revelation was also made (Eph. 3:3-5). Emphasize that, although Luke traced out the course of the life of Christ from those who personally were eyewitnesses from the beginning, he was also guided by the Holy Spirit and, thus, wrote accurately (2 Tim. 3:16-17).

Give the class a good background understanding of the purpose and content of the books of Luke and Acts. Show how they were both

Notes

addressed to "Theophilus" which means "a lover of God," and point out that we do not know whether this was a man who then lived or Luke's way of personifying all men who loved God, thus addressing his writings to them. If you have time it would be good to read the first four verses of Luke and then from the last chapter to show its beginning and end. Then read from the first chapter of Acts to illustrate how they connect together chronologically.

Conversion of Lydia

Many practical lessons are to be learned from Lydia. Show how Luke was with Paul and Silas in this city of Philippi. Although he does not mention himself as speaking, we know that his presence must have involved him somewhat in the conversion of Lydia and her household. Discuss Lydia, her home, business, and devotion to God. A good incidental point to make is that she came to worship God even though she was away from home on business. Illustrate that some today do not have this sort of devotion. Such devotion is necessary, for we must always put God first whether at home or away, whether in business or not (Matt. 6:33).

Discuss the specifics of her conversion and how they coincide with every other case of conversion recorded. There was preaching done, she believed, and was baptized. You may have a question about infant baptism since Lydia's household is often used as evidence of infant baptism. Point out that the text does not even say she was married, for the word "household" often included only the servants. But furthermore, if she were married, there is no proof she had children. If she did have children, we could not prove they were infants. And if there were infants, we could not prove she had taken them with her 300 miles away from home on a business trip. Indeed there is too much assumption here to used her conversion as proof infants were baptized in New Testament days. Every other case on record where the word "household" is used it is also said they "believed"; therefore, they could not have been infants.

Check the exercises to see how well the class has studied and learned the lesson.

Lesson 9

Aquila and Priscilla, A Devoted Couple

Begin the class by briefly reviewing "Luke, The Beloved Physician."

When You Complete This Lesson You Should Know

Of Paul's work with Aquila and Priscilla in tentmaking. Paul went into Corinth without financial backing. He labored with his own hands and established a great church. Until we have the spirit of self-denial and sacrifice which will make us willing to do the same thing, we can hope to accomplish but little so far as evangelizing the whole world is concerned. Financial backing is good, but not essential to evangelizing the world.

About their teaching Apollos. We are to be as wise as serpents and harmless as doves. Priscilla and Aquila exemplified such wisdom in their handling of Apollos. Had they challenged him publicly on his preaching, they might never have reached him with the truth.

Of their courage and faith. True friendship shows itself in sacrifice for our friends. Priscilla and Aquila proved their friendship for Paul when they willingly laid down their necks, or exposed themselves to the danger of losing their lives, in order to save Paul from death.

The Scripture Text describes the first two sections of the lesson and should be read or put in your own words at the beginning of the lesson to set the background for drawing these aims of the lesson. The memory verse is from the third section. Therefore, the teacher should wait until discussing the courage and faith of Aquila and Priscilla before having the class to repeat this from memory.

Paul Meets Priscilla and Aquila

Use the map to point out where Corinth was located and that Paul came there from Athens. Corinth was not the home of Priscilla and Aquila either. They were from Pontus and had recently come from Rome because the emperor had made all the Jews leave.

You may discuss the fact that they were tentmakers and if you have a good encyclopedia or commentary that has a picture of the type of tents they made, it would be interesting. Just as Paul supported himself, men who preach today should be willing to do the same. You may also want to point out that it is God's will to that preachers be supported by the church as Paul was at times (1 Cor. 9:9-16; 2 Cor. 11:8; Phil. 1:3-5; 4:15-18).

Priscilla and Aquila Teach Apollos

Again point out from the map that Priscilla and Aquila left with Paul and went to Ephesus where they stayed for a while. Read Acts 18:24-28 about Apollos and explain that he was an eloquent man and mighty in the Scriptures. Discuss the baptism of John, pointing out that it was once commanded of God and that even Jesus was baptized by John (Matt. 3:1-17). However, after the death of Christ, people were to be baptized in the name of the Lord (see Acts 19:1-7). Apollos evidently

Notes

had not been taught about Christ, for he received the teaching with the right attitude and "mightily convinced the Jews" when he knew the full truth.

Perhaps you will want to expand on the thought introduced into the lesson about the place of the woman in teaching a man. The Bible does not condemn a woman for teaching a man, but rather for teaching "over" a man. Her place is that of subjection but, in that place, she can still teach a man who is willing to learn.

Paul Salutes Prisca and Aquila

The name Prisca is but a diminuitive form of the name Priscilla. You may want to read or at least tell about the danger Paul faced in Corinth (Acts 18:12) and later at Ephesus (Acts 19:23) as you discuss the courage of Priscilla and Aquila who risked "their own necks" for Paul. Apply the lesson to the students by encouraging them that, should we ever be faced with the choice of death or Christ, we must choose Christ which will give eternal life. We need courage in standing for the truth (Acts 4:19-20 5:29, 41-42).

Discuss also the "church that is in their house," showing that the "church" is not a building, but people who are saved. Also, show that Christians sometimes met in homes and that we must not feel that a building is a necessity in order to worship God. If we are ever in difficult fields where there are few Christians and no buildings in which to meet, we should gladly conduct worship in our homes.

Lesson 10

Apollos, the Eloquent Preacher

Begin the class by briefly reviewing "Aquila and Priscilla, A Devoted Couple."

When You Complete This Lesson You Should Know

The Bible does not give us much detail about the life of Apollos. If he ever travelled with Paul on any of his journeys, it is not recorded. Although he was not one of Paul's closest companions, Apollos was a fellow-laborer and their lives were both indelibly marked on the church at Corinth. Therefore, it is fitting that we study about Apollos in this series of lessons.

These three aims of the lesson should be easily developed. All three of these points are drawn from the Scripture Text, so early in the lesson you should have the class read the text and keep their Bibles opened there for the discussion. The memory verse fits best in developing the third point so wait until that time to drill the class.

In the beginning of your class you should remind them of the fact that Aquila and Priscilla were left in Ephesus by Paul at the close of his second journey. Point out on the map where Ephesus is located; later you will want to show that Paul returned there (Acts 19) and taught the twelve men.

"An Eloquent Man, Mighty in the Scriptures"

Have the class define the meaning of "eloquence" and discuss questions (1) and (2) in the exercises regarding the necessity of eloquence in preaching. Make the point that eloquence is not essential to preaching the gospel in power, but also allow the fact that it is a wonderful gift, if properly used.

Discuss the other traits of Apollos that made him such an excellent preacher. It was not only because of eloquence, but also because he knew the Scriptures, was fervent, and diligent. Try to draw your class into a discussion of these qualities and see if they can think of a man in their own knowledge who possesses such traits. Indeed, such a man is rare, and that point will show just how powerful Apollos really was.

Knew Only the Baptism of John

As you discuss this section, you will definitely need to bring in the events of Acts 19:1-7. Make a clear distinction to the class that, at one time, the baptism of John was approved of God but that, by the time of Acts 19, its purpose had been served and therefore its practice was unlawful. Depending on the maturity of your class and the depth of their understanding, you may want to get into a discussion of the baptism of John (Matt. 3:1-17; Mark 1:3-5). John's baptism was for remission of sins, but it could provide such only in anticipation of the shedding of the blood of Christ. This is why they were commanded to believe on Christ that should come after John. This was the mistake of Apollos and the twelve men from Ephesus—they had not been taught of Christ,

Notes

although as many as twenty or more years had passed since He had ascended into heaven.

The major point to be learned as an application for our own life is that not just any baptism is acceptable to God. It does matter what a person does religiously (Matt. 7:21; 15:7-9; Luke 6:46). Many claim to have been baptized, but it is not of Christ. Here are some misunderstandings of baptism: sprinkling (instead of immersion), infant baptism, baptism because sins have already been forgiven, baptism to become a member of a denomination, etc. This is a good time to teach what is the baptism of Christ and its importance.

Paul Planted, Apollos Watered

Show on the map where Apollos went from Ephesus, particularly teaching that Achaia is a region, not a city. Achaia was the Southern portion of what is called Greece today. Tie together Acts 18:27-28 with 1 Corinthians 3:4-11, showing that the work of Apollos in the city of Corinth had truly been effective. Discuss what Paul meant by the expression that he had planted, Apollos watered, but God gave the increase. Apply this to preaching that is done today by several different men. Also draw the lesson that Paul is making in teaching against division, particularly in becoming followers of men. While we may all have men we love to hear preach better than others, we must avoid "preacher-itis" or a spirit that separates and causes jealousy. Make the point that preachers are but men, servants of God, and must not be elevated as though they are the Lord themselves. They must be humble and so must all brethren.

Lesson 11

Onesimus, the Runaway Slave of Philemon

Begin the class by briefly reviewing "Apollos, the Eloquent Preacher."

When You Complete This Lesson You Should Know

The purpose of this lesson is to familiarize the student with the book of Philemon and the unusual purpose for which it was written. The three aims set forth can all be accomplished without leaving the Scripture Text; in fact, the best preparation you can make as a teacher will be with a good commentary on the book of Philemon. Be well acquainted with the whole chapter.

The memory verse is more in the line of an application of the lesson rather than an integral part of the lesson proper. It would probably be best to discuss the Scripture Text verse by verse and then work the exercises in order. When you come to the last exercise ("Lessons Learned from Philemon"), you may want to expand the thoughts introduced and invite class discussion. At this point of the lesson, the memory verse will best fit as a point in showing how God's law changed the attitudes of servants and masters but did not automatically release them as servants. Use all of Ephesians 6:5-9 to show that masters were commanded to maintain the proper attitude toward servants, even as God is no respecter of persons.

Paul Pleads for a Slave

This section is designed to make the student use his Bible rather than depending on the lesson book altogether. The thoughts from this section are contained in verses 8-12. You may develop the background by describing conditions during the time of slavery—men were actually owned by others. Point out that Philemon could have taken the heathen attitude and would have had the civil right to punish Onesimus even to death for having left him. Point out on the map the distance from Colosse to Rome, explaining that we have no record of how or why Onesimus ran away, nor do we know how he got to Rome. But the fact that, in this condition, he was willing to hear the gospel and "take the risk" of returning to slavery shows the power the gospel has over those who obey it, both slaves and masters.

"Above a Servant, a Brother Beloved"

This section of thought is a discussion of verses 13-16. For Philemon to receive a slave—especially one who had run away—in the spirit Paul requested required a deep faith in God. Many times in our own lives we must work to maintain the ideals of heaven even when others around us have wronged us in time past. It may be that the sorriest person in town obeys the gospel, but even so we must forgive and count him as a brother.

Whether rich or poor, black or white, the gospel makes us one in Christ. This is a good place to develop the point that the gospel is not for certain classes of people and that we must be humble (Jas. 2:1-8; Rom. 12:9-10, 16; John 13:34; Matt. 20:25-28).

Notes

Philemon's Debt to Paul

This section of thought is taken from verses 17-21. Tie in the thought we learned in our last lesson that we must not be followers of men or lift up preachers above one another (1 Cor. 3:4-1 1), yet at the same time those who have taught us the gospel have rendered a great service which we cannot repay. Philemon had this sort of debt to Paul. Therefore, Paul requested that he regard the debt owed to Paul when he began demanding the debt Onesimus owed him. In fact, Paul had such love for Onesimus that he was willing personally to pay whatever debt was outstanding. In the truest sense we all owe God the greatest debt and, if He is willing to forgive us our wrongs, we certainly must forgive others when they sin against us (Matt. 18:23-35).

You may want to have the class to read the verses used in the last exercise and even add to them others which teach the same lesson. Get them to explain how or why they think these lessons are found in Philemon. Ask them for other lessons to be learned and make the application to their own lives as to whether or not they are obeying these lessons.

Lesson 12

Women Who Helped Paul

Begin the class by briefly reviewing "Onesimus, The Runaway Slave."

When You Complete This Lesson You Should Know

The background for this lesson will be women Paul mentioned as having labored with him in the gospel. But the primary lesson we wish to put across to the students is the important role and responsibility of women in the Lord's church. Perhaps not enough is said to teach from a positive point of view what women can and must do. We often hear what they are not to do—i.e., preach, serve as elders, usurp authority over man, etc.

Students of Junior age level usually have high ideals and identify with some idol, whether he be a star in sports, entertainment, or some other field. Now is the best time to make characters of the Bible become real to them and to impress the students with the need for being like God wants. In previous lessons we urged the young men to consider preaching the gospel like Timothy, and in the next lesson we stressed the need for developing themselves to serve as elders of a church. In this lesson, we want to devote special attention to the young girls that they may realize that God has an important work for them just as He does for the boys. From a positive approach we want the girls (and boys too) to know that their role of subjection to man is not one of inferiority but simply a different responsibility, that both men and women must work together to accomplish greatness in God's sight. Also, we want them to understand the practical application of the lesson by discussing some of the important works women can do in serving Christ.

Work Women Can Do

This lesson is designed so that the exercises will provide opportunity for good class discussion. You will probably want to start the class by setting forth the fundamental theme as described in the section "Work Women Can Do" and then proceed rather quickly into the exercises. The first three exercises are directly related to the Scripture Texts, so you may have these read to the class and tie them together with the context of study for this whole quarter, i.e., Paul's companions. Emphasize that what they did was important and, even though they are not remembered as preachers, yet they "labored" and their names are written in the Book of Life.

The last two exercises are for general teaching and application of the work women can and should do. You may find it profitable to discuss briefly each of the ten scriptures as they are used to answer the True-False questions. Also this is a good time to have the class quote the memory verses as they are both used in the exercise. Urge the class to discuss their answers for the last exercise and to give practical applications of our lesson. A good finish to the lesson should be the description of a virtuous woman in Proverbs 31:10-31. Try to leave a high ideal with the students and urge them to be content with God's way and happy for their work.

Notes

Begin the class by briefly reviewing "Women Who Helped Paul."

When You Complete This Lesson You Should Know

One of the safeguards against falling away from the faith is to be taught that such is possible and, in fact, has occurred in the past. The object of this lesson is to inform our students of some who have left the faith to teach them about some of the ways these men departed and how we can be guilty of the same. Then we want to build a support under our students for such times in their lives when they see others depart. Too often brethren have become discouraged and quit the faith because of others. We need to keep our eyes on Christ, for if our faith is in Him, then the action of other men should not make us cease living right.

Departing from the Faith

So much is said these days about the "hypocrites in the church." Frankly admit that there may be hypocrites in the church; there were in the first century (Acts 5:1-11). But God dealt with them then and He will judge the modern hypocrites. Use this point to emphasize that Paul did not hide behind the hypocrites, nor did he use them as an excuse for indifference. No doubt he was disappointed in these men, but Paul continued faithful to the end.

As you go over the verses for which they are to fill in the blanks, you should emphasize that the Lord knew some would be unfaithful. These scriptures foretold of some who would depart. Another point is the solution in our own lives to guard against such: 2 Timothy 3:5, "from such turn away" and Hebrews 3:12-13, "exhort one another daily." Emphasize the need for constant companionship of faithful Christians. You may find it a good time to talk about the need to choose our friends (1 Cor. 15:33). Also, stress the need for faithful attendance to all the services "that we may provoke one another to love and good works" (Heb. 10:23-25).

Demas Hath Forsaken Me

We cannot define exactly what Demas loved to cause him to forsake Paul. It could mean the sinful things of the world, for we often speak of worldliness and have in mind such things as drinking, gambling, fornication, etc. But Demas may have simply lacked the courage to stand by Paul for fear his own life might be taken. We just do not know. However, whichever sense is meant, Demas was in the wrong. The exercise for matching verses is to cause them to think about things of the world that are right within themselves, You may take some time to talk about the idea of worldliness as mentioned above, but also impress upon them how good things can be made sinful if we let them come before our service to Christ. Provoke the class to discuss the choices Christians must often make in life: choices involving education, goals in life, business, etc. And give them practical illustrations about how these choices all must be made considering whether we can remain diligent servants of Christ. Many a Christian has been lost to the Lord because he chose a job (right within itself), but his job consumed his time and energy so much that he became indifferent to the faith.

This section of study is the most appropriate time to test them on the memory verse.

Shipwreck of the Faith

Show the class that we can depart the Lord by false doctrine as well as through unrighteous lives or indifference. Hymenaeus and Alexander were delivered so they may learn "not to blashpheme." Make the point that simply because we once know the truth and obey it does not guarantee that we will always be faithful. We must constantly study and test the preaching we hear. Several passages can be added here in thought (1 John 4:1; 2 John 9-10; Acts 17:11; 2 Cor. 11:14-15; 2 Thess. 2:10-12). We must not follow what men say because we like the man, but rather because he gives a "thus saith the Lord" (1 Pet. 4:11). The crossword puzzle should serve as a summary to the overall thoughts of the whole lesson.

The Purpose and Nature of Miracles

A Word to the Teacher

Few studies could be more important to you and to your class than a study of miracles. It is important, first, because of the serious misconceptions that are common. These misconceptions tend to opposite directions. Many deny that miracles have ever occurred. Others insist that they can now be performed if men have sufficient faith. It is urgent that such misconceptions be corrected if they have begun to develop and that children learn the truth which will guard them against these errors in the future.

Second, in a positive way, the understanding and appreciation of miracles is essential to faith. Faith is the foundation on which all else that is pleasing to God must be built. The children you are teaching are at the age when such faith must be developing. In God's providence, they are at an age when miracles are most interesting to them. Their active minds make it possible for them to participate in the events they study.

Your task is to help them develop this understanding and appreciation of miracles, and a challenging task it is! You will accomplish it not only by what you say, but by what you are as you share your faith with them (2 Tim. 1:5). Pray to God each day that He will help you to accomplish your task. And remember, if you succeed, it may well be one of the most significant achievements of your life.

Supplementary Material for Your Use

Any good reference books will be useful to you in preparation of these lessons. If the teacher has none, the following would be useful for any teaching done in the future:

Eerdman's Bible Handbook
The New Smith's Bible Dictionary
Zondervan's Pictorial Bible Dictionary
The Zondervan Pictorial Encyclopedia of the Bible (5 vols.)
International Standard Bible Encyclopedia (5 vols.)

An old scholarly work on the subject of miracles is *Notes on the Miracles* by Richard C. Trench and another work is *The Miracles of our Savior* by William Taylor. A more popularly written work which contains many of the thoughts of Trench is *All the Miracles of the Bible* by Herbert Lockyer, published by Zondervan. We would particularly recommend this book for the average teacher. James Bales' book, *Miracles or Mirages* is particularly helpful in understanding that miracles are not to be expected today.

Time-Line Project

It is urgent that students obtain some concept of Bible history. These lessons on miracles provide a good opportunity for teaching this since they cover the entire period of revelation.

Use three walls of your classroom (or four if necessary) to cover the centuries of Bible history. Usher's chronology, though of doubtful accuracy, will serve to establish the relationships. Cut out forty-two small pieces of paper (about 2" x 4") and label them with a marker to represent the centuries, beginning with 4,000 B.C., then 3900 B.C., 3800, etc. Continue past 0 to 100 A.D. These should be spread out as far as space will permit along the walls of the classroom as near the ceiling as possible. They may be attached with masking tape or some other substance which will not leave a mark on the wall. In attaching these, be sure to leave a space before the year 4,000 for the creation.

For this first lesson, cut out four more pieces of paper, longer than the above, and label them for the special periods of miracles: EXODUS, ELIJAH / ELISHA, CAPTIVITY, and CHRIST/EARLY CHURCH. Place EXODUS under the years 1500 and 1400 B.C.; ELIJAH/ELISHA under the years 900 and 800; CAPTIVITY under the years 600 and 500, and CHRIST/EARLY CHURCH under 0 and 100.

Later, you will be placing each miracle in its proper location. It would be difficult to overestimate the value of this exercise. It will do much to help the children remember these periods and their relation to each other. It will also impress upon them that there were many centuries when no miracles occurred and this will prepare them for the fact that none are being observed today.

Purpose of This Lesson

This lesson is planned to help the students understand the concept of miracles. It is not enough to say that miracles are an event contrary to nature. Miracles are the introduction into our world of another force superior to nature. This force may actually use nature, but in such a way that supernatural influence is clearly evident. The story in the beginning is designed to help explain this.

Some Things You Should Know

At the beginning of each lesson there is a list of things which the student should be able to do when he has completed preparation of the lessons. These are designed to challenge the students and to give them goals toward which to work. Their immediate reward will be your approval.

In this first class period the teacher should help the students to memorize the definition of miracles if they have not done so. You will have occasion to refer back to it again and again. Drill the students also on the periods when miracles were performed.

Some Questions to Help With the Definition of Miracles

Is an eclipse a miracle? Why?

If the newspaper should report that three inches of snow fell in Miami or Los Angeles, would this be a miracle?

Was it a miracle when men walked on the moon? Why?

If a high school football team defeated a college team, would this be a miracle? Why?

Answering the Questions

Question number 2 can best be answered using the New King James Version (or KJV). Answers are wonder, signs, miracles.

Notes

Assignment For Next Lesson

Assign one of the better students to prepare a report on *evolution*, telling what the theory involves and how it contrasts with the Bible account of creation. This should be ready for the next class meeting.

Lesson 2

Creation

Purpose of the Lesson

Miracles are displays of God's power. The creation is the ultimate such display. Throughout Scripture, God is magnified as the God of Creation. Your purpose should be, not only to acquaint your class with the facts of creation, but to thrill them with the significance of it; to help them to stand in awe before the God who possesses such power; to encourage true and reverent worship before Him during the class, in the assembly, and even in personal devotion.

To encourage such a spirit of reverence and awe, you as a teacher must possess it. Give diligence to develop it. Pray God to help you. Try to arrange the time immediately before the class period so that there will be no hindrance to a keen awareness of God's greatness and of His presence. See that your students see nothing in your life inconsistent with such a manifestation of reverence.

The teacher should make certain that the three kinds of power exhibited in creation are clearly in mind: (1) Power to make something from nothing. (2) Power to make order from disorder. (3) Power to make life from non-life. Find illustrations of your own to help impress these concepts.

Take to Class

Material for Time-line. Cut a piece of paper on which you will write CREATION with a marker. Have masking tape or double stick tape available with which the children can attach the word CREATION to the wall before the year 4,000.

Material for Assignment. Prepare ten pieces of paper, each with one of the ten plagues written on it, as follows:

Nile turned to blood – Exodus 7:14-25
Frogs – Exodus 8:1-15
Lice – Exodus 8:16-19
Flies – Exodus 8:20-32
Murrain – Exodus 9:1-7
Boils – Exodus 9:8-12
Hail – Exodus 9:13-35
Locusts – Exodus 10:1-20
Darkness – Exodus 10:21-29
Death of Firstborn – Exodus 11 and 12

These will be given to the children as assignments for reports in the next class meeting. You will find that they will come much nearer to doing them if you give them the assignments written on paper.

Suggested Class Procedure

Review: Be sure the students remember the definition of miracles. Review also the purpose of miracles.

Notes

Illustrating Power. Ask the class to give examples of each kind of power. They will be glad to name some athletes who possess physical power, some men who use their minds to accomplish things with machines, and men who have political power. A few words may well be said to show that each of the students may exercise moral power whether they have other power or not.

Report on Evolution. When the class has discussed God's making life from non-life, have the report on evolution. You can show that the whole concept of evolution is based on the possibility of life coming from non-life without intelligent supervision. This is contrary to all known laws of science. How much more reasonable it is to believe that an omnipotent God created life than to believe that it created itself!

Concluding the Lesson. This is the point where the matter of worship should be emphasized. Have the students quote the memory verse individually and then in unison. Then ask for suggestions of hymns that praise God for His creative power. If hymn books are available and it can be done without disturbing others, sing the hymns together, emphasizing the words. The following might be suggested:

Worthy Art Thou
Hallelujah Praise Jehovah (Note verse 2 especially)
This is My Father's World
The Spacious Firmament on High

If these cannot be sung in class they may be read aloud.

Lesson 3
Crossing the Red Sea

Purpose of the Lesson

This lesson beautifully demonstrates the impossibility of successful resistance to God. Here we see God against Pharaoh, against the magicians, against the gods of Egypt, and finally against the army of Egypt. Any one of these was a formidable foe. Each may have seemed for a time to have some advantage over God, but each was eventually humiliated and defeated.

Your students are often subjected to anxieties growing out of their exposure to the fears of the adult world. Assure them that the same God is with them if they are faithful to Him. He does not now work miracles but, as seen in the lesson, He could have done all He did without miracles. The miracles were simply to show His power that Israel might trust Him and that we might have faith that He can take care of us.

Take To Class:

A concordance

Three pieces of paper for your Time-line exhibit. Label these: FLOOD, PLAGUES, and RED SEA CROSSING

Suggested Class Procedure

Review: Definition of miracles, Purpose of miracles, Three ways God's power is shown in Creation.

Lesson links: Give the children a quick review of Bible history from the creation to the Exodus. Make use of your Time-line to indicate the flow of the story. Place FLOOD between 2400 B.C. and 2300 B.C. As you tell of Abraham, tell that he lived about 1900 B.C. Then bring them quickly through Isaac, Jacob, and Joseph to Egypt. Go ahead and place the PLAGUES and RED SEA CROSSING markers under 1500 B.C. on the Time-line.

Have the reports on the plagues. Take as little time as possible while discussing the major facts.

Ask the two reasons for the plagues. Check answers to the questions regarding plagues. (E, F, A, D, C, B)

Have one of the children tell the story of the Red Sea Crossing, or tell it yourself.

Check answers to the questions under II.

Ask for three things accomplished by the crossing of the Red Sea: (1) Israel was delivered from Egypt. (2) Israel was impressed with God's greatness and power. (3) Israel's enemies in the promised land were intimidated by knowledge of what God had done to the Egyptians.

Check to see if the children can say the memory verse. This verse is important to show the spiritual value of the miracle. You might compare it with John 20:30, 31. God was giving evidence of approval for Moses.

Notes

Discuss the thought questions.

See who found the verse saying the waters were congealed (Exod. 15:8). Ask how it was found. Demonstrate the use of the concordance or an online Bible. Look under the word "congealed."

Assignment: Assign two students to make oral reports in the next class meeting. In paragraph three of the next lesson you will find miracles listed which took place between the Red Sea Crossing and the giving of the manna. Have one report on the sweetening of the bitter waters (Exod. 15:22-27), and one on Water from the Rock (Exod. 17:1-9).

If any time remains, use it to re-emphasize God's care for us. Have the children list things about which they are concerned. It may be the political situation, economic situation, or a military crisis in the news. Show that these are no greater than the problems faced by Israel. God does not have to reveal Himself to us; we know Him. He does not have to give approval of Christ as His messenger; this has already been done. So, we need not expect a miracle; we can expect Him to take care of us through natural means.

Lessons 4

Miracles in the Wilderness

Purpose of the Lesson

Two great thoughts should be in your mind as you study and teach this lesson: (1) That miracles are intended to teach lessons. (2) The lesson taught by this particular miracle is that God can care for His own if they are faithful to do His will. Your students are beginning to feel the tensions and stress of the world about them. This lesson, like lesson 3, can help them develop trust in God. Remember that your own faith will be the most effective factor in helping them to develop trust in God.

Take To Class

A piece of paper for your Time-line marked QUAIL-MANNA.

A reference Bible.

Suggested Class Procedure

Ask the children if they have taken a bus trip of several hundred miles or, perhaps, a camping trip involving a large number of persons over several days. Let them tell some of the problems. Then let them help you describe the wilderness and the size of the Israelite nation. Let each one write down on a paper three or four problems he would expect. Then write down the various ones suggested on a chalk-board.

Show how God helped solve all of these problems. Remind the students that God helps us solve our problems, too. Give special attention to the solving of the food problem and place the words, QUAIL-MAN-NA, on your Time-line.

Go through the questions on Exodus 16 under "The Manna."

Between discussion of "The Manna" and "Lessons God Taught Israel with the Manna," go back and review the definition of a miracle. Note that it is "an unusual act of God, performed as a sign which men can observe, but can neither explain nor perform themselves." Give special emphasis to the fact that it is "performed as a sign." Remind them also of the designations: miracles, wonders, and signs. Ask them how the manna was each of these. They should know that it was a *miracle* because it demonstrated the power of God. It was a *wonder* because the people were amazed. It was a *sign* because it taught a lesson, it proved something. When this is impressed, go ahead to the discussion of "Lessons God Taught Israel With The Manna."

Answers to Lessons God Taught Israel with the Manna

1. God taught them not to eat too much by having them gather only an omer (about 3 qts.) for each man and working it so that none had more than this.

2. He taught them to trust Him for daily bread by forbidding any hoarding of the manna.

3. They had to get up early because it would disappear when the sun was up to warm it.

Notes

4. They were taught to respect the Sabbath by gathering a double portion on Friday so that they would not have to gather on the Sabbath.

5. To place a jar of manna in the ark of the covenant.

Answers to Lessons For Us

1. Phil. 3:19

2. Matt. 6:11

3. 2 Thess. 3:10

4. Rev. 1:10

5. 1 Cor. 11:23-26

Some Questions for Discussion in Class

If we are taught these things in the scriptures, do we need a miracle to teach them to us?

When we obtain our food, is it from God? Does the fact that we have to work for it make any difference in this? Did the Israelites have to work for theirs?

Here we see that God is doing for us without a miracle what He did for them with one. He is teaching us the lessons through His word and providing our food through nature.

Suggestions on Thought Questions

(1) If the substance falls from the trees only during one or two months of the year, it was not the manna. Furthermore, it would not have fallen six days a week and not on the Sabbath, nor would it have kept over Friday night but spoiled every other night. There would not have been enough trees to feed Israel. But if all of this had worked out this way, it would have been beyond the usual working of nature and would be a miracle anyway. It would simply mean that God was using these trees as instruments of the miracle.

(3) God must have taken away the manna when they arrived in Canaan because they could then provide for themselves. God never does for us what we can do for ourselves.

I CHALLENGE YOU. Show the children how to use a reference Bible. Deuteronomy 8:3 should refer to Matthew 4:4 and Luke 4:4. This memory verse is long. Help the children to learn it, stressing that Jesus learned it.

Assignment

Assign two reports for next week: One on the Jordan River and one on the city of Jericho. Good reports on these can be obtained from a Bible dictionary or even from an encyclopedia.

Lesson 5

The Conquest of Canaan

Purpose of the Lesson

This lesson provides another opportunity to stress that miracles were intended to build faith. Both the crossing of Jordan and the conquering of Jericho could have been accomplished without miracles, but Israel might have learned only to trust in themselves, not in God. God wanted them to believe in Him and this explains the use of the miracles. This cannot be stressed too often in this series of lessons for it is the key to understanding why miracles are not being performed now. Other means are available for producing faith.

Take to Class

Strips of paper for your Time-line marked SINAI, NADAB/ABIHU, MIRIAM'S LEPROSY, EARTH SWALLOWS REBELS, BRAZEN SERPENT, CROSSING JORDAN, and WALLS OF JERICHO.

A Bible dictionary and a reference Bible.

Prepare nine assignment slips to be given to students.

"The Widow's Oil" (1 Kings 17:9-16)
"Raising the Widow's Son" (1 Kings 17:17-24)
"Elijah Taken to Heaven" (2 Kings 2:1-18)
"Jericho's waters sweetened" (2 Kings 2:19-22)
"Oil increased" (2 Kings 4:1-7)
"The Shunamite's Son" (2 Kings 4:8-37)
"Naaman cleansed" (2 Kings 5:1-14)
"The Floating Axe-head" (2 Kings 6:1-7)
"Syrian Army Blinded" (2 Kings 6:8-23)

These reports are to be made in the next class meeting.

Lesson Links

Plan to give your students a brief account of some of the events in the forty years of wilderness wandering with emphasis on the miracles. You should study to be able to tell the stories of the miracles for which you have prepared the paper for the Time-line. You will find these as follows:

Sinai - Exodus 19-20
Nadab and Abihu - Leviticus 10:1-7
Miriam's Leprosy - Numbers 12
Earth swallows rebels - Numbers 16
The Brazen serpent - Numbers 21

Practice telling these stories so as to make them as interesting as possible. As you tell each story place the title of the miracle on the Time-line under the years 1500 to 1400. It will now be evident that this period saw many miracles.

Tell of the death of Moses and of Joshua's accession to the role of leader. Stress that the people entering Canaan were a much stronger

Notes

people than those who left Egypt forty years earlier. They had seen many miracles. The miracles had increased their faith.

Suggested Procedure for Class

Have the report on the Jordan River which you assigned last week.

Go through the answers to the questions from Joshua 3.

Drill the class on the four things accomplished by the miraculous crossing of Jordan, beyond the mere relocation of the marchers from one side to the other. Let the students suggest other ways they might have gotten across Jordan.

Discuss the character of the Canaanites. Impress on the class that they had been wicked and were unworthy of the land. God had waited until they had proved their unworthiness before driving them out (Gen. 15:16). Later, when Israel forgot God they, too, were removed from the land. No people have a right to a land when they forget God (Ps. 9:17).

Have the report on Jericho assigned last week.

Go through the answers to questions on Joshua 6:1-10.

Show your students how to use a Bible Dictionary and /or a reference Bible to find that Elijah and Elisha crossed Jordan on dry land after separating the waters (2 Kings 2:8,14).

This reference to Elijah and Elisha will be a good introduction to the next lesson. Give out the assignment slips to the children, being sure to give the longer ones to the better students.

Make certain the children can repeat the memory verse. Use any time left to show them how the faith of the Israelites obtained for them the victory over Jericho only when their faith led them to obey God.

Lesson 6

Elijah Calls Down Fire From Heaven

Purpose of the Lesson

God developed Israel's faith as a nation by miraculously bringing them out of Egypt, sustaining them in the wilderness, and establishing them in Canaan. In this lesson, however, that faith is being seriously diluted by the heathenism of surrounding nations, encouraged particularly by Israel's queen, the idolatrous Jezebel. Complete loss of faith would jeopardize God's plan for bringing Jesus into the world through Jacob's line. God's response is an unusual series of miracles performed by Elijah and Elisha. These miracles are not so much to preserve Israel as a nation as to preserve Israel's faith.

God never leaves His people without sufficient grounds for faith. His word now produces faith. It is sufficient for the purpose. As the attacks of infidelity have increased in recent years, no new miracles have been wrought, but by God's providence increasing evidence has been uncovered to strengthen the hand of those who contend for the faith. This has served to accomplish what would have required miracles in an earlier age. If it be objected that not all are convinced, note that not all were convinced by the miracles. This is clear in this lesson.

Take to Class

Ten strips of paper for your Time-line. Label one for each of the miracles assigned for report and one for FIRE ON MOUNT CARMEL.

A map showing the divided kingdom, Mt. Carmel, and Jezreel.

Any Bible dictionary or atlas where you have found the distance from Mt. Carmel to Jezreel.

Assignment slips to be given out for next week. Reports on:
- The three Hebrew children – Daniel 3
- Nebuchadnezzar's life among the beasts of the field – Daniel 4
- Daniel in the lions' den – Daniel 6

Lesson Links

Some five hundred years intervene between the last lesson and this one. Begin the class with a quick review of those years. If you are developing the Time-line, follow it as you give the survey. Between 1400 and 1100 tell them of the Judges. Just before and after 1000, tell them of Saul, David, and Solomon. Between 1000 and 900, the kingdom is divided. On the map show the northern and southern kingdoms. This lesson is between 900 and 800 B.C. Elijah and Elisha prophesied in the northern kingdom.

The following fact should be stressed: Many miracles were wrought during the lifetime of Moses and Joshua. But between them and Elijah, there were very few miracles. This should help the students to accept the fact that no miracles are being seen today. God only works miracles when there is a special need for creating faith. This is accomplished today, as already noted, by His word.

Notes

Supplementary Preparation

In a Bible atlas or dictionary learn all you can about Mount Carmel and its position relative to the sea and Jezreel. This will help you to bring alive the story of the contest and, particularly, the coming of the rain.

Suggested Class Procedure

1. Do your introduction as suggested in Lesson Links.

2. Discuss Jezebel and her god, Baal.

3. Discuss Elijah's first confrontation with King Ahab, announcing the drought.

4. Go through the questions from 1 Kings 18:17-46.

5. Discuss the thought questions.

Some advantages of Baal's prophets: They outnumbered Elijah, they had first opportunity, they were on a high place which was supposed to be special to Baal, the contest involved fire which was Baal's peculiar instrument, they were given choice of the animal to be sacrificed, etc.

Pouring water on the sacrifice proved Elijah was not using hidden coals or similar devices to deceive.

In killing the prophets of Baal, Elijah was following God's law. Stress that, although we are not to punish false teachers physically, God expects us to deal firmly with error. See Titus 1:10-11 and Romans 16:17. Discuss the seriousness of false teaching.

6. Have reports (assigned at previous class meeting) on the other miracles of this period. Be sure you know the stories in case a student is absent or unprepared.

7. According to *Eerdman's Bible Handbook*, the distance from Mount Carmel to Jezreel is seventeen miles. If you found it in a reference book show the children how you did it. Ask how they found the answer.

8. Make the assignments for the next lesson. Encourage study of the interesting stories for the best possible presentation.

Lesson 7
The Handwriting on the Wall

Purpose of the Lesson

In this lesson, Israel is once again in a foreign land and God is working miracles to preserve their faith in Him. But God is not appealing only to His people; He is creating faith among their captors. Here you can show that Bible miracles convinced unbelievers. So-called miracles claimed today are believed only by those who already believe in the claims of the miracle-workers. Emphasize the great impression made on the Babylonians by these miracles. They were convinced of the power of Israel's God, even against their will.

Take to Class

Four strips of paper for the Time-line labeled with the miracles described in Daniel and assigned for reports.

A map showing Babylon in relation to Jerusalem from which the Jews had been taken captive.

Supplementary Preparation

Read the first six chapters of Daniel. Do some study on Babylon, the city and the empire. This will serve you well in this lesson and in the next as well. From 2 Chronicles 36, read of Babylon's conquest of Judah and the deportations. From Bible dictionaries, handbooks, or any set of encyclopedias, read of Babylon's fall.

Lesson Links

Go back to the last lesson to remind your students of the purpose of the miracles in the days of Elijah and Elisha. Show them, however, that the effect was only temporary. Israel continued to serve idols until God allowed them to be taken away into captivity, never to be re-established as a nation.

Judah, however, was also worshipping idols. If they were destroyed as a nation, God's promises to bring Jesus into the world through Judah could not have been fulfilled. An idolatrous nation would not be prepared to receive Jesus. So God allowed Judah to be disciplined, defeated, and carried into a foreign land. This served to separate them from the idolatry of Canaan. At the same time, by miracles, He kept them aware of His power and of His concern for them.

Suggested Class Procedure

1. Go through the introduction as suggested by Lesson Links.

2. Tell the story of the fall of Jerusalem and the deportations to Babylon. Use the map to describe the distance and difficulty of the journey. Tell what you know of Babylon. Daniel was in the first deportation. Tell of his early life in Babylon, the honor offered, his conscientious refusal to eat the "king's dainties," and the result.

3. Have the reports which were assigned on the three Hebrew children and on Nebuchadnezzar's experiences among the beasts.

Notes

4. Go through questions on Daniel 5:1-4.

5. Have the students read their newspaper reports of the writing on wall.

6. Discuss the influence of Daniel in the court. Why was he so well-known.

7. Discuss answers to the questions on Daniel 4:17-31.

8. Thought Questions:

Here is a good opportunity to warn against alcohol. Besides the sin of drunkenness itself, there are sins into which individuals are easily led under the influence of alcohol. The very first effects of alcohol are on that part of the brain which makes moral judgments. These judgments are difficult enough to make when the brain is clear. When wrong judgments are made, the fact that one is under the influence of alcohol does not provide escape either from the guilt or consequences of the sin.

Here is an opportunity to warn against profaning the Lord's name, the Lord's supper, the Lord's day, etc.

Belshazzar's conscience must have been hurting. He knew his conduct was not proper.

By this miracle God made Belshazzar and all Babylon and the Jews aware that overthrow of the city was His doing, meted out in punishment for its sins.

Today, people trust in scientific technology, industrial power to produce, sophisticated military equipment such as bombs and missiles, or sheer weight of numbers of personnel or equipment. All of these will prove as vulnerable as Belshazzar's wall if a nation's sins cause God to determine its destruction.

9. Have a report on Daniel in the lions' den. Note that this is under the Persians.

10. Discuss the memory verse. This is a good time to review the definition of miracles, signs, and wonders.

11. For next week, ask students to find pictures of the present sight of Babylon. Have them check magazines and encyclopedias.

Lesson 8

Prophecy Is A Miracle

Purpose of the Lesson

This lesson should be used to stress the fact that the Scriptures are not the product of human wisdom. The Bible is the product of a Divine intrusion into the world of men, just as are all other miracles. Without a miracle there could be no inspired scriptures.

As noted in this lesson, prophecy is more than mere prediction — more, even, than inspired prediction. It is a man speaking God's mind. The wisdom and knowledge are supernatural. But the supernatural is most evident when God infallibly predicts the future through these men. Prophetic prediction, then, becomes one of the strongest proofs of the divine origin of the Bible.

Most miracles were observable only to a limited number of observers. But prophecy is a miracle, the result of which can be observed by us today. We have the Old Testament prophecies which we can see fulfilled in the New. Furthermore, we can read the predictions of the destruction of great cities in the Old Testament. We can go to the site of those cities, see the evidence of their former glory and at the same time the fulfillment of the prophecies of their abandonment. The very pictures of Babylon which the children should bring should be used to impress this.

Lesson Links

The scene of our last lesson was Babylon. Many of God's people had been taken from their homeland into that distant land. God was concerned for the faith of His people. As noted in the last lesson, there was a danger that both the Jews and Babylonians might interpret the Babylonian victory as evidence of the weakness of Judah's God. We saw that God worked miracles to display His power so that even the king of Babylon had to confess: "His dominion is an everlasting dominion, and His kingdom endures from generation to generation. And all the inhabitants of the earth are accounted as nothing, but He does according to His will in the host of heaven" (Dan. 4:34-35).

But God did more. He sent prophets whom He enabled to speak for Him. These prophets spoke to God's people wherever they were. Daniel was God's prophet in the courts of the Babylonian and Persian kings, Ezekiel was among the captives in Babylon, and Jeremiah was among those few who remained in Jerusalem. These were interpreting the captivity, predicting the return of God's people and the overthrow of their enemies.

Suggested Class Procedure

Introduce the lesson with Lesson Links above.

Ask for a full definition of prophecy. Be sure to stress that it goes beyond mere prediction. It includes all that the prophets said for God.

See that the class can quote the memory verse. Discuss it.

Notes

Discuss detection of false prophets. Stress that we do not have to wait to see if his predictions come true, for if he acts or speaks contrary to what an acknowledged prophet has taught, he is false (see Deut. 13:1-2). All who claim prophetic powers today fail on this point.

Discuss Hananiah and Jeremiah and answers to questions in the lesson concerning them.

Discuss Isaiah's prophecies concerning Babylon. On your time-line, show that Isaiah lived in the 700's. The captivity was in the 500's. It was in the 300's that the city was abandoned. The prophets prophesied the abandonment of other great cities (e.g. Tyre, Ezek. 26:3-14) and complete destruction of other great nations. But no such prophecy was made concerning Egypt (see Isa. 19:16-24). If the prophecies concerning the other nations had been mere human guesses, surely the same fate would have been predicted for Egypt.

Discuss the matching questions concerning Isaiah's prophecies of Christ.

Supplementary Exercises: Have students turn to Psalm 22, which was written 1,000 years before Christ was born. Have them list as many allusions to Christ's crucifixion as possible. See how many references they can find to Christ in Isaiah 53.

Discuss the Thought Questions.

I CHALLENGE YOU: Revelation 22:18. Discuss the implications of this verse in evaluating modern prophets (?).

Lesson 9
The Virgin Birth and
Resurrection of Jesus

Purpose of the Lesson

The miracles of this lesson are two of the most important of all history. They were performed, not so much to produce faith as to accomplish what could never have been accomplished through natural means. Yet, they are the strongest possible supports of faith. Without the virgin birth and the resurrection, we could never believe in Jesus as the Son of God. This fact is the cornerstone and foundation of all faith.

Stress the importance of these miracles. Make it clear that the students will encounter professed Christians who will deny these miracles. These modernists may contend that one may accept Jesus as a great teacher and profit by His life without accepting these fundamental miracles. You must prepare your students to "Stand Up for Jesus." If these events did not occur, Jesus was an impostor, unworthy of respect.

Take to Class

Strips of paper for your Time-line, marked VIRGIN BIRTH and RESURRECTION.

Lesson Links

Except for inspired prophecy, the last recorded miracles of the Old Testament were those during Daniel's lifetime. This was in the late 500's B.C. At this point, such miracles ceased. Inspiration continued fifty to seventy-five years longer and then prophecy ceased. And so, for approximately 500 years, there were no miracles. God had said all that He needed to say and His word had been confirmed by miracles.

This period of no revelation and no miracles is comparable to our own. God was clearly working among men. His hand was to be seen in the lives of Ezra, Nehemiah, and Esther. But, except for the inspiration of the books, His working was providential, not miraculous. The people of that period would have been foolish to deny the miracles of the Old Testament because no miracles were being worked in their day. And we will be foolish if we reject those of the Old and New Testaments just because no miracles are being worked today. God's word has been given and confirmed.

Our period of no miracles will be broken by the second coming of Jesus. That period was broken by His first coming.

Suggested Class Procedure

Introduce the lesson with Lesson Links above.

Have students repeat the memory verse. Why should Jesus be called Immanuel, "God with us"? Was He God? This study may well raise the question of the Godhead. Use of the word "Deity" in place of God might be helpful in understanding. The Word was not the Father, but the Word was Deity, just as the Father was Deity. The Holy Spirit was also Deity. Yet, there is but one Deity.

Notes

As a comparison to "one Deity" made up of Father, Son, and Holy Spirit, compare to mankind. Although there are billions of "men" (mankind), all have the same nature—there is one mankind. In the same way that there are billions of people with the same nature, there are three persons who have the one nature of deity.

For practice, take the position that Jesus did not exist before He was born of Mary. Let the students convince you that you are mistaken.

Answer questions on Luke 1:26-35.

Discuss Christ as our mediator. In dealing with this section, stress the fact that although God was angry with man because of his sin, God still loved man even when man did not love God. It was God who took the initiative and provided the mediator. Be sure the students understand the connection between the virgin birth and Christ's qualification for meeting our need.

Suggestions for BE A DETECTIVE

If Jesus was never really dead, how did He survive the cross, particularly the spear? How were the Roman soldiers fooled into thinking He was dead? How could He have rolled away the stone from the inside, especially in His weakened condition?

If enemies took the body, what was their motive? How could they overpower the guard and break the seal? Why did they not produce the body when the disciples began preaching the resurrection?

If friends took the body, what gave them the courage to undertake the theft? How could they have overpowered the guard? Why did not one of them admit the hoax when it became clear that they would be persecuted and even killed for preaching the resurrection?

Place the miracles, VIRGIN BIRTH and RESURRECTION on the Time-line.

Assignment: Have students bring to class a list of all the miracles of Jesus. They will find such a list in many Bibles or in a good Bible handbook.

Lesson 10
Miracles of Jesus

Purpose of the Lesson

This lesson considers a very small sampling of the wonderful works of Jesus. The miracle of feeding the five thousand is the only one recorded in all four records of the life of Christ. It has been the one most often twisted by rationalists in an effort to explain away the miraculous. All of this suggests its effectiveness in creating faith. Pray that God may help you to impress your class with its magnitude so that their faith in Jesus may be increased.

Take to Class

A map showing the Sea of Galilee

A picture of the Sea of Galilee

A long strip of "butcher paper" at least nine to twelve inches wide to be placed on the Time-line. Have this attached below the words VIRGIN BIRTH and RESURRECTION which were placed there in the last lesson. You will also need a felt-tip marker.

Suggested Class Procedure

Begin the class by asking how many children have brought the list of miracles performed by Jesus. Let each one call out one until all have been named. As each one is named, place it on the "butcher paper" with the marker.

Discuss the list of miracles briefly. Go through the list, designating those that involved healing of physical and mental disorders, those proving power over nature (including the two being studied in this lesson), and those involving raising of the dead. Ask if any of these involved any selfish motive.

Jesus refused to perform two miracles that were proposed by Satan (Matt. 4:1-7). Why did He refuse? Would these have been for selfish purposes? Whose faith would have been strengthened by turning stones to bread? Emphasize that creating faith was the purpose of all the miracles that He performed.

Go through the questions under "Feeding the Five Thousand." Some claim that everyone had actually brought a lunch with them into the country to hear Jesus. But they were all afraid to bring out their lunches, not knowing that others had brought one and fearing that, if they brought one out, it would be taken from them. It is said, however, that when Jesus proposed to feed all with the small lunch, they had enough faith in Him to believe He could do it and so every man brought out his own lunch and ate it. If this explanation were correct, what would it indicate about Jesus' honesty? Is it possible that the disciples would not have known what was happening (see Matt. 14:19)? If they knew the above had happened and reported it as we have it in our text, what does this tell us about their honesty?

Notes

Go through questions under "Another Miracle." In this connection show the location of the Sea of Galilee on the map and show any pictures you may have of it.

THOUGHT QUESTIONS: Did Jesus announce that He would feed the multitude so that they would come to hear Him preach? How long did He allow the 4,000 to follow Him before He fed them (Matt. 15:32)? Do churches today ever use food and other earthly enticements to encourage people to attend services? Is this following the example of Jesus?

Have the students repeat the Memory Verse. Discuss the significance of it. Some say that some of the unrecorded miracles of Jesus were performed in His childhood. Ask your students' opinion of this. Then settle the question with John 2:11.

Discuss the questions under "Results of the Miracles." Emphasize again the importance of the miracles to us in convincing us of Jesus' Sonship and of His concern for man's physical needs. If questions arise concerning the miracles, remind the students that the disciples were permitted to observe His miracles closely. They could not have been deceived in the others any more than in the feeding of the 5,000. They could not have been deceived and their willingness to die for their testimony is proof they were not deceivers.

Lesson 11

Miracles in the Beginning of the Church

Purpose of the Lesson

This lesson should be used to show how God's power was used to bring the church into existence. No human institution has ever experienced such a beginning. Use this to help the students to appreciate the church. There is another important lesson that should not be overlooked. The church was ushered in by miracles just as were the heaven, earth, plant and animal life in the original creation. But after the original creation, further miracles were not necessary. Even procreation of life is by natural means. So it is with the church. No miracles are now needed such as were performed on Pentecost.

Take to Class

Strips of paper for the Time-line marked H. S. BAPTISM, TONGUES, DEATH OF A. & S., HEALING, APOSTLES' ESCAPE.

A map showing places from which people came to Jerusalem on Pentecost. *Eerdman's Bible Handbook* has a splendid map for this purpose on page 551. One may also be available on the internet.

If available, get a recording of some modern "tongue speaker."

Lesson Links

The last lesson showed how Jesus' works bore witness that He was sent from God (John 5:36). In this lesson, Peter states that Jesus was "approved of God among you by miracles and wonders and signs which God did by Him" (Acts 2:22).

But when Jesus sent forth His apostles into all the world, they had no written message from Him. They had to remember what He had said and then convince others that they were presenting His message accurately. This called for further miracles. Before He died, Jesus promised the Spirit Who, He said, would provide miraculous recall of what He had said to them as well as future revelation (John 14:25-26). After His resurrection, Jesus promised them the power to work miracles in connection with their preaching of the gospel (Mark 16:15-18). Mark 16:20, which was the first memory verse in this series of lessons, records the fact that, as they went forth, their words were confirmed by signs following. Hebrews 2:3-4 states the same. This lesson contains the first of those miracles.

Suggested Class Procedure

Introduce the class study with the Lesson Links above. Be sure to take the opportunity to review the students on the memory verse from the first lesson, Mark 16:20. Discuss the two miracles of Pentecost: Baptism of the Spirit and Tongues. Place these on the Time-line.

Use the map to point out the various places represented in Jerusalem on Pentecost. See how many different languages of that period can be named.

Notes

Go through the questions under "The Miracles of Pentecost." Check the answers.

If a recording of some modern day tongue speaker could be obtained, it would be an interesting experience for the students. (Check the internet for someone speaking in tongues.) If any are troubled by the thought that we should be speaking in tongues, the teacher should point out that many unbelievers today claim the same power. Those that are practiced today have no distinctive evidence to offer for divine guidance. The teacher would do well to read *Glossolalia, From God or Man?* by Jimmy Jividen, published by Star Bible Publications. Remember, also, I Corinthians 13:8.

Have a good student tell the story of the Apostles' escape from prison. After the telling of the story, go back with the class and read it.

Place these miracles on the wall under the Time-line.

Lesson 12

Miracles in the Spread of the Church

Purpose of the Lesson

The last two lessons in this series offer a fine opportunity to climax the whole series. With the background which the students have now gained, they should be able to understand why miracles were so much needed in the early days of the church, but not needed now. You should emphasize again and again that the primary purpose of the miracles was not to accomplish the immediate end, such as healing of the sick or casting out of demons, but rather the development of faith. Now, with the written word, miracles are not needed for this purpose.

This lesson shows clearly how the power to work miracles was given — by the laying on of the apostles' hands. With no apostles today, it is clear that no such powers can be expected.

Take to Class

1. A good map of Judea and Samaria.

2. A strip of paper for the Time-line labeled IMPARTING GIFTS. Lesson Links

Our last lesson described the beginning of the church. The apostles were quite active in the affairs of that church and provided the miraculous powers that were needed. But as the church spread and there was still no written New Testament, the miraculous powers were needed wherever new congregations were formed. This lesson describes the use of those powers and describes how they were transmitted to those who were not apostles.

Suggested Class Procedure

Introduce the lesson with the Lesson Links above.

Try to picture the problems of carrying on the work of the early church without a written New Testament:

- Who would know what to preach?
- When one preached, how could he prove that what he said was so? If a disagreement arose, how could it be settled?
- If a stranger came in claiming to be a prophet, how could they know whether he was genuine or false?
- How could they convince unbelievers of the truth?
- If an unbeliever was contacted who spoke only a foreign tongue, how could he be taught?
- If a teacher spoke in a foreign tongue, how could he be understood?
- If new Gentile converts had to meet Jewish Rabbis in discussion how could they compete with their knowledge of the Old Testament? How could new converts have wisdom to make proper decisions in the church?

Notes

Today, with the New Testament available as it is in all languages, these problems can be solved. There was no way to accomplish these things in New Testament times without miracles.

Use the map to describe the spread of the church, especially into Samaria.

Go through the questions under "Philip's Work in Samaria." Here several of the problems above were solved because Philip possessed the miraculous gifts.

Under "Counterfeit Miracles," emphasize the fact that the true miracles of Philip were altogether superior to those of Simon. Many different religious orders today claim to work miracles. Most of these insist that they are the only ones performing true miracles and that all others are false. Yet, the ones they brand false are just like their own. In this they condemn themselves, for if their own were true and the others false, theirs would be as superior to the others as Philip's were superior to Simon's. Also, if theirs were true, those accepting the false ones would see the superiority of the true ones and would make the same change that Simon's disciples made.

Under "Special Gifts," stress the fact that Philip could not pass on his powers. This could only be done by apostles. Question 4: Simon tried to buy the power to lay his hands on others that they might receive the Holy Ghost (v. 19).

Learn all that you can about the nine gifts of 1 Corinthians 12:8-10. Discuss these with the students. Go back to the questions under #2 of these Suggested Class Procedures and ask those questions again. Let the students tell which of the gifts would help to solve the problem posed by the question.

Place on the Time-line IMPARTING GIFTS.

I CHALLENGE YOU: Acts 19:6

Assignment: Urge the students to review all of the lessons on Miracles and be ready for a test next class meeting.

Lesson 13

True and False Miracles

Purpose of the Lesson

It is hoped that this lesson may help students to develop a wholesome skepticism toward professed miracle workers. When they have learned this lesson properly, they should be able to give good reasons for rejecting the claims of all such men today.

Take to Class

I. A strip of paper for the Time-line labeled LAME MAN HEALED.

2. A copy of the test for each student. Make your own test if you prefer.

Suggested Class Procedure

You will have to use your time very carefully to have the class finish the test. Go immediately into the questions under "True Miracles Are Superior to False Ones," comparing true and false miracles.

Raise this question: If a person did perform a work which seemed to pass all the tests proposed, or even raise the dead, should one then believe just anything he said? In discussion of this consider Deuteronomy 13:1-3 and Galatians 1:8-9.

2. Go through questions under "True Miracles Confirm True Teaching."

Discuss "True Miracles Are Worked by Authorized Men." Has God anywhere promised us the power to work miracles? Has He authorized us to perform them? Could we do them in Jesus' name? Is it possible that some may be deceived into thinking that they themselves are performing miracles?

Place LAME MAN HEALED on your Time-line. Now, you are ready to bring into focus your patient use of the Time-line. It will be well worth the work you have done. Review the four periods of miracles. Show that these were periods of revelation and special crisis of faith. Show that there were periods of hundreds of years when no miracles were being performed. We are in such a period now. We need no miracles because we have God's complete revelation and it has already been confirmed.

The fact that there are no miracles now should not deter us from trusting God for help. Remember Nehemiah and Esther. They were greatly helped by God, but not miraculously. It can be so for us.

Test

1. Tell what a miracle is.

2. Name four periods in Bible history when miracles were most common. (Note to teacher: Before the test begins, you may remove these from the Time-line, or you may leave them there and give the children these points.)

Notes

Match the following:

_____ 1. Miracle which "magnified Joshua in the sight of all Israel: and they feared him as they feared Moses."

_____ 2. Miracle which caused Israel to believe the Lord and in His servant, Moses."

_____ 3. Miracle which proved God was superior to Baal.

_____ 4. Miracle which was the first and greatest display of God's power in the Bible.

_____ 5. Miracle which taught Israel that man shall not live by bread alone.

_____ 6. Miracle which made it possible for Jesus to be both God and man.

_____ 7. Miracle which proved that Jesus Son of God.

_____ 8. Means by which early Christians the Spirit miraculously.

_____ 9. Miracle which occurred the day the church was established.

_____ 10. Miracle which showed that God directed the defeat of Babylon.

A. Resurrection

B. Virgin birth

C. Laying on of the apostles' hands

D. Baptism of Spirit

E. Handwriting on the wall

F. Contest on Carmel

G. Crossing Jordan

H. Manna

I. Red Sea Crossing

J. Creation

IV. True-False

_____ 1. Miracles happen every day.

_____ 2. The only way God can do anything is by a miracle.

_____ 3. It required a miracle to give life to what was not alive.

_____ 4. The plagues showed God's power over the gods of Egypt.

_____ 5. God's miracles caused the rulers of Babylon to respect Him.

_____ 6. Prophecy is always a prediction of what will happen in the future.

_____ 7. Jesus existed as the Word before He was born.

_____ 8. Jesus is God with us.

_____ 9. When Peter and John healed the lame one could deny the miracle.

_____ 10. The only purpose of Jesus' miracles of sick people well.

www.ingramcontent.com/pod-product-compliance
Lightning Source LLC
LaVergne TN
LVHW081319060426
835509LV00015B/1581